THE Crochet Crowd

INSPIRE · CREATE · CELEBRATE

Macintyre Purcell Publishing Inc.

Michael Sellick & Daniel Zondervan

MacIntyre Purcell Publishing Inc.
194 Hospital Rd.
Lunenburg, Nova Scotia
B0J 2C0
(902) 640-3350

www.macintyrepurcell.com
info@macintyrepurcell.com

Printed and bound in Canada by Friesens

Cover and book design: Tanya Montini
Cover photo and select interior images: Heidi Jirotka

ISBN: 978-1-77276-160-3

Library and Archives Canada Cataloguing in Publication Title: The Crochet Crowd : inspire, create & celebrate /
Michael Sellick and Daniel Zondervan. Names: Sellick, Michael, author. | Zondervan, Daniel, author. Identifiers:
Canadiana 20210166762 | ISBN 9781772761603 (softcover) Subjects: LCSH: Crocheting. | LCSH: Crocheting—
Patterns. Classification: LCC TT820 .S45 2021 | DDC 746.43/4041—dc23

MacIntyre Purcell Publishing Inc. would like to acknowledge the financial support of the Government of Canada and
the Nova Scotia Department of Tourism, Culture and Heritage.

NOVA SCOTIA

Funded by the Government of Canada | Canada

THE

Crochet

Crowd

INSPIRE ✦ CREATE ✦ CELEBRATE

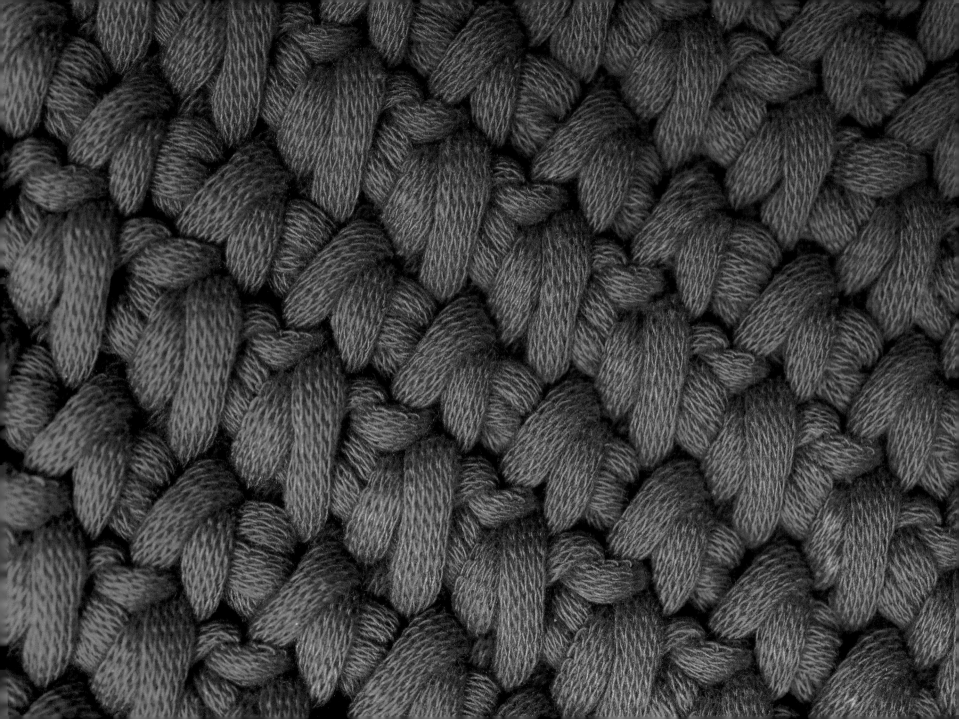

A special thank you to all friends and mentors who have helped us accomplish some of our wildest dreams and ideas, including shows and live events. To all those working behind the scenes providing online support, we wouldn't have this opportunity without you.

Table of Contents

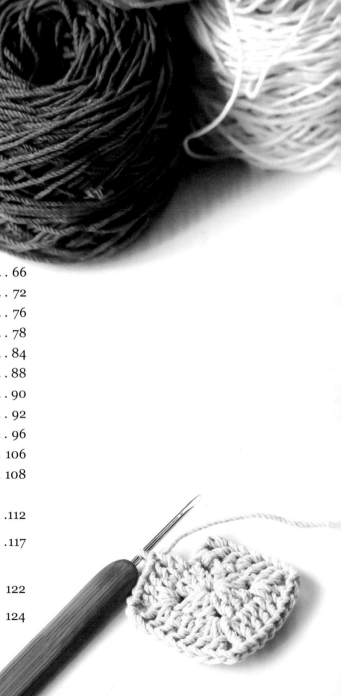

Introduction

Hey there, Mikey from The Crochet Crowd here, so grab your hook and yarn and let's play. While you're at it, pour yourself a little drinky. Although this stitch story is primarily about my stitching journey, it's really a story about this amazing community that since 2008, (that's 70 in PuppiDawg years), has supported us, taught and nurtured us.

Was this a road to become a celebrity? The answer is NO. It's been a journey marked by a HUGE love for yarn, as well as hard work, and some very thick skin.

The first steps of this adventure started when I found the centre of a yarn ball and it just so happened I was a truck driver looking for ways to keep myself from feeling unwanted on the road.

Crochet gave me goals. It gave me a mission to create something. Having something to do with my hands allowed me to address my feelings and cope with whatever else was happening in my life.

Crochet can be as simple as a granny square, or it can stump you like textures and cables sometimes do. But it's oh so satisfying and comforting, like the calming feel of finger-pleasuring yarn as it runs through your hands. Ahhhh... And unlike so many other things in life, it is forgiving; if you make a mistake, it's easy to unravel and start over.

The Crochet Crowd has grown a lot from when I was doing crochet tutorial videos in my spare time. When I began, I only had 10 videos. Now, we have 3,000 videos on our *YouTube* channel. That's a lot of inspiration.

I felt compelled to teach but didn't know how to until I discovered the power of outreach through *YouTube*.

We are so proud of and grateful for the online crochet community. With more than 1.3 million followers on *Facebook*, a million subscribers on *YouTube* and 150,000 on *Instagram*, we are constantly inspired by you. And to think this all started because I wanted to find and be a part of a community.

To be able to create from our home in a small community in Nova Scotia's beautiful Annapolis Valley makes this even more special.

Our guiding principle is that everybody should be able to learn and that educational resources should be free. We also wanted the learning to be fun and uncomplicated so that beginners could easily absorb and master the basic skills.

We encourage you to be yourself, have a few laughs,

make some new friends, and, most importantly, crochet to your heart's content, or at least until the dessert table is empty.

If you're new to us or already know us, we hope you enjoy our story and the patterns we've included. This is our first book, and we've tried to capture the fun of what we've been doing online and in person for more than a decade. We are always striving to evolve to meet the challenges of an online community and technology advancements. We are a WIP (work in progress).

We feel pretty lucky to do what we do and to have the amazing community we have. We've done a lot of work on the patterns in this book, going for a range of things you can make for your family and your home.

So, hang on. This isn't just a pattern book. This is for our community who's always wanted to know my story. Happy reading and happy hooking!

Mikey and Diva Dan

(and Puss Puss, Binky Boo and PuppiDawg)

Learning to Crochet – Michael's Story

First Steps

When I was a teenager, walking into a yarn store for the first time made me feel out of place and awkward about asking for yarn.

"Are you buying this yarn for your mom?" the cashier would inevitably ask. My heart would sink, and I'd say, "No, it's for me." Stereotypes have a way of choking off your internal joy.

I felt like I was buying stuff that I wasn't supposed to be buying. Some kids were trying to sneak peeks at Playboy (or Playgirl – duh). But here I was, feeling furtive because I wanted to make something pretty.

Throughout my teenage years and up until The Crochet Crowd began, I wouldn't reveal to many people that I knew how to crochet.

I kept at it though. I just did what I had to and still enjoyed crochet, even though it was my own little secret. Crochet helped quiet my mind by making me concentrate on one stitch at a time. While I don't like the saying that I crochet so I won't kill people, this hobby was a lifeline for me at the right time in my life. For others, they crochet just because they can; for me it was deeper.

Crisis of Confidence

I grew up in a home where creativity was encouraged and daydreams were gateways to ideas.

Living for a short time in a small town in Ontario, arts and crafts were a way to fill time in the evenings, while the wood stove heated our cottage in the cold winter months, and my mom looked for something else to fill our time besides watching television.

As a little kid, I was really into crafting — particularly weaving on a loom. My Grade 4 teacher was passionate about weaving and she brought her loom to school to show us and let us practice. I was so captivated that when we had activity time, the loom was the go-to. I would think of all the different things I could do with it. My young brain was sparked by the creativity of yarn. Creativity with yarn rules!

I was so driven by it that I asked my parents to buy me a loom and they did. I had visions of making my own scarves and I did it with a joy I still remember. I used leftover yarn from my mom. My scarves were nothing spectacular, but they were made by me.

Gratified by the process and excited by this new potential, I took my loom to school to show my teacher.

Even though the box featured one girl and the loom was bright pink, I didn't care. But my classmates did, and one kid snapped it in half. It was at that moment that I realized yarn arts are marketed towards a gender that isn't my own, even though I loved it so much.

I was defeated and pushed back into the closet to keep my passion quiet. Life changed and we moved to a big city to follow my dad's job. Living in a large metropolis was an eye opener and a catalyst for self-assessment. I realized it was not just yarn where I was out of place.

If you haven't gone through it, it may be hard to grasp, especially these days when there are so many more supports and allies for LGBTQ+ youth. Back then I was in a small town with nobody to talk to about how I was feeling, which was isolated and alone. I'm not even sure I would have known how to articulate it. But I knew I was different. I knew I just didn't fit.

I had taken so much joy in the yarn arts when I was younger. As a bullied teen, I reflected on my younger years and on what brought me joy. I lost my will to live and couldn't figure out my contribution to society. This world is a tangled ball of yarn, eh!

The Breakthrough

When I was 14 my mother taught me to crochet. She let me find my way with the hook and yarn. There was no pressure. My mother understood the ways I needed to learn.

"Wrap the needle and insert it into the hole and then wrap again … pull out from the hole," she would say. "Wrap the needle again, and pull two loops on the needle, then wrap the needle again and pull through the last loops."

By the end of the evening, I was loving the concept and it ignited a new beginning. It changed my life.

The next day, I went to the store to buy my first hook and a bag full of blue variegated yarn to do a full-size blanket. I was hooked big time.

At school, I would daydream about going home to crochet. At night, I would crochet in front of the TV completely entranced by the craft. In a couple of months, I had my first double-size afghan done. Yep, even with a *fancy-dancy* double crochet border.

Crochet Saved My Life

My mother taking the time to teach me acted as suppression and redirected my mind from suicidal thoughts. Crochet, for me, wasn't just a skill, it was a coping mechanism. It basically saved my life many times over.

Having the experience as a bullied, introverted kid, you domino yourself into being invisible, and you feel isolated and devalued. So, I found a way through the help of my mom to channel my feelings into crochet instead of hurting myself. I'm not sure where I'd be without it. It was the thing I could rely on when my life hit the skids.

Crochet for me is personal. It's a healing mechanism. It's therapy.

That's why we've worked so hard to make The Crochet Crowd a welcoming, supportive community. I know there are people screaming for help, but they can't be heard. That was me. I turned to crochet when I was in need.

I want our community to be that kind of lifeline, where creativity can help us push through. As much as our community is there for others, it also helps me.

The Crochet Crowd satisfies my own need for community as I see value in reaching out to others who may be just like me and in need of a friend where crochet is the conversation.

Chucking It All

Crochet helped me cope with school and was my constant companion as I went on to graduate from college with a diploma in mechanical engineering, design technician. Even though crochet was my passion, it never occurred to me that it could ever be a career. I had been working since I was 14, and basically supporting myself since I was 18.

But by 2003, I had just turned 30 and wondered what I was doing with my life. You know what I mean. You examine your job, friends, goals and why you are eating endless boxes of Kraft Dinner.

Like many people who hit that age, I realized my life wasn't what I thought it would be. I then had a job at a factory in Barrie, Ontario, that gave me anxiety attacks and made me miserable. I had property and keepsakes from my marriage that had ended years earlier.

Yes, I followed the straight path, and that may surprise you. Coming to terms with being gay, smack-dab in the middle of a marriage, was one of the worst moments in my life. I knew something wasn't right; I couldn't put my finger on it and rushed to marriage because I felt that was expected of me. I lacked the courage to speak up for myself at the risk of hurting another person. In fact, I did more psychological damage to my family, and more importantly, to my wife. My fear was unforgivable for the emotional mess I created for her. To anyone living with doubt in your life, I speak frankly to you: you have one life to live, be honest with yourself and to those around you.

I purged everything I owned and did a life memory dump. eBay was the flush I needed. I sold everything I owned for less than 200 bucks! I didn't care about money; I just wanted it gone. I discarded what items I had left from my childhood and donated them to the local dump. I love a good purge and the cleansing that goes with it!

On the Road ... and Online

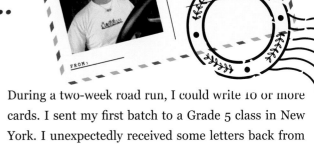

In the midst of the midlife crisis, a new, unexplored and unexpected chapter began. I started seeing someone new. He taught me how to drive a transport truck and I ended up driving a truck for three years before plunging into The Crochet Crowd full time.

My partner and I would drive together. Basically, I would drive at night and he would drive through the day. We had long-haul routes all over North America, but our main routes were to Texas, Oregon and Arizona. It wasn't all smooth driving. There was some grinding of the gears and trust me when I say I'm not great at backing up. We saw the ugly and the beauty during these years.

Big Road Dispatches: A Crochet Crowd Prelude

To put my trucking time to good use I joined a program called "Trucker Buddy," which paired participants with an elementary classroom. The idea was that I would pick up postcards along my route and write stories about my travels.

During a two-week road run, I could write 10 or more cards. I sent my first batch to a Grade 5 class in New York. I unexpectedly received some letters back from the students telling me about them and asking me questions.

Writing to the kids helped give me a newly found sense of belonging and a feeling that I mattered. They actually wanted to hear from me! I needed this kind of contact in my life. I figured I would take this one step further and write letters to each student too. It began several years of relationships with the same teacher and her classes. Eventually, younger siblings of the students in that first class would also write to me. I was their writing assignment.

But for me, they were pieces of the world that were missing in my life. Those kids will never really comprehend that they were my "call a friend" lifeline at a point in my life where I was lost.

Being in the program taught me that community isn't just about who lives near you. It's the people you embrace and who become part of your world, whether in person or online like The Crochet Crowd. It's truly a privilege if someone allows you to participate in a life.

Michael  Mikey

During the first year of the Trucker Buddy program, Tyra Banks was hosting *America's Next Top Model.* The show had a segment called Tyra Mail. Since the show's contestants were so excited about getting Tyra Mail, I thought we could be special just like her.

Because of privacy concerns, the kids would sign their letters to me with only their first names. So, I pitched the idea of having the students sign their last name as "Mail." For example, I heard from Tyron's Mail, Ayesha's Mail, and so many more. My name was Mikey's Mail.

It was in my final year in the program that I learned about *YouTube.* I thought to myself, 'What if I sent videos to the classroom? I could virtually put the students in the driver's seat.

I started to put videos on *YouTube* about the places I visited on my truck routes but soon realized that the students couldn't access them because *YouTube* was banned at the school. I filmed underground in SubTropolis for example, a huge artificial cave in Kansas City, Missouri, where an old mine was converted into what's called the world's largest underground storage facility.

Bottom line, I created a *YouTube* account with the username Mikeyssmail. This is the same account we use today for The Crochet Crowd. If you follow us on *YouTube*, have you ever noticed the URL for our channel: youtube.com/user/mikeyssmail? I didn't realize it would be my permanent username.

OK, hold on, I know what you might be thinking. Why not just create a new channel? Well, by this time my crochet videos were gaining followers, so when we came up with a name The Crochet Crowd years later, we didn't want to start fresh and lose our followers and community. So, ta-daa! I was doing crochet videos as Mikey's Mail. Hey, it's not always rocket science.

Little did I know, though, that when I created my *YouTube* account to reach kids in New York City, I was setting up the next stage of my journey.

Oprah Calling

One day in 2008, when my relationship was rocky, out came my yarn to deal with my racing mind. I was watching the Oprah Winfrey Show. It was just another lazy afternoon crocheting away on the couch.

But something Oprah said changed my life. (I know a lot of people say that, but it's true!) She was talking about finding your journey and your purpose in life. Basically, if something in your life is broken, find a reason to change it, and find gratitude.

From Oprah's mouth to my ears: she made me realize that everyone has a calling in life. Even me.

As I sat there hooking with Oprah, I thought about how I couldn't grasp the crochet tutorials on *YouTube*. I'm sorry, but almost all of the videos were boring. I thought if I felt like that, maybe there were others out there like me. I wondered to myself (as if my mom was in the room), 'What if I were to do it differently? What would I do?'

I zoned out as Oprah was talking and looked down at my project and thought, "What if I taught this on *YouTube* using the words my mother would use to teach me?" Bring out my balls and dare to be different. Flip the concept, get off the soapbox and just immerse myself into a community.

Mind blown, people!

Camera: Check.

Hook: Check.

Yarn: Check.

Sorry Oprah, I love you, but you got turned off halfway through the show.

I sat on the floor of my living room. No sound equipment. No fancy introduction with music. No introduction to myself. I just wanted to be me, from my language to my presentation skills. I spoke like an everyday crocheter speaking to another everyday crocheter. Nothing elite to see here.

"Let me show you how to do a single crochet."

Just me offering something to the world. It was that basic! Never underestimate the power of simple ideas.

I was so motivated that I filmed 10 videos based on stuff I already knew. I did have something to offer the world, and that was teaching a skill the way I learned it. I didn't know if it would go anywhere. I didn't know if anybody would watch.

But I knew this is what I had to do. It felt right.

My partner left nine months after I got started but I had been playing with my camera and started a new journey while my relationship was collapsing which really knocked me for a loop. A journey that would eventually take me to a different mindset and start a global community down the road. You know, bad things can inspire new things!

Enter Diva Dan

I met Daniel Zondervan three months before Mikeyssmail (later to be The Crochet Crowd) hit one million views on *YouTube*.

When we met, though, I didn't want to tell him about doing crochet videos in my spare time. My previous partner didn't want me on *YouTube* because he thought it was a violation of our privacy, and he wasn't wrong about that.

Pretty soon, I spilled my dirty little secret, and he immediately encouraged me to do more. He took me to Len's Mill Stores, a craft and surplus stock outlet in Ontario. It was the first time I had been in a "real" yarn store. And it was amazing. Although, I could have been high on yarn fumes too!

Imagine meeting somebody where a date included a yarn store. Yep. It was love at first sight. I mean balls to the walls! What's not to love? Daniel is my equal. He's the guy who picks me up when I'm getting attacked online. He's the guy that slaps me across the head (lovingly, I think) when I've done something stupid. And he's the one who encouraged my creativity, to make me see that I could go further.

Daniel: The Backstory

Daniel grew up on a farm in rural Ontario where his parents and extended Dutch family raised dairy cattle and pigs and planted 1,000 acres of cash crops. It wasn't an idyllic life. Daniel was like me in that he felt isolated, but what he did find was a passion for music and gardening.

His mother developed schizophrenia while on the farm and a parental divorce soon followed. He was uprooted to Walkerton to finish high school. He went on to study music at Wilfred Laurier University majoring in viola but also studied harpsichord and pipe organ.

At the same time (Daniel was still away in university), his mother's struggles with schizophrenia had escalated and she was moved to a group home for her own protection. Daniel became the surrogate parent in dealing with police and working with doctors to get her help.

Jumping ahead — and trust me, it's a book of its own — Daniel went through obstacles and life experiences and he brought that richness to our relationship.

Isn't It Ironic

Daniel says it was ironic, but when he first met me, I was afraid to be creative. One of the first things he said to me was let's do a painting together. Neither of us knew how, but we bought this huge six foot by four foot canvas. One half was his and the other half was mine. The whole point was for each of us to paint something of personal significance.

I was so afraid to pick up that paint brush. And one day, something just clicked, and I started painting like there was no end to it. And then Daniel did his. When we looked at it, we realized all the colours and the lines complemented each other.

That painting hangs in our workspace, just outside the studio where I do my videos and other work. Looking at it now, it's like it was painted by one person. You can't see where his part of the painting ends and mine begins.

19

"Inviting and inclusive."

Stitch Journey Starts Here

In 2010, we were set to go to our first Creativ Festival in Toronto, Canada's largest crafting show. We went as a vendor but were also invited to teach loom knitting and crochet at one of the live instruction booths, but believe it or not, we still didn't have a business name. Our *YouTube* channel was still called Mikeyssmail. Our *Facebook* business page didn't exist. I was using my personal profile page. In today's era, that sounds prehistoric.

Our first show! We were so excited but Daniel had a thought. How would people get to know us on the internet and at the show with a name like Mikeysmail? Light bulb: name change coming.

We love to brainstorm, so off we went. We wanted to play off the word "crochet," of course, but also off the idea of community. I came up with "The Crochet Clique," but that was too exclusive and Daniel suggested "The Crochet Crowd."

That was it! It was inviting and inclusive. We wanted to create a welcoming community of crocheters where people could share the joy of crocheting with other people who are just as passionate as we all are. I added our slogan Inspire, Create & Celebrate, and we've been doing just that with The Crowd ever since.

CREATIV Part 2

Attending the Creativ Festival and changing our name to The Crochet Crowd changed the direction of our future in what seemed like a split moment of time. In April 2011, after five years with the trucking company, I quit my job. I realized there was the possibility that I could support myself through *YouTube* tutorials and devoted all my time to The Crochet Crowd. It was scary as hell. Thank gawd Diva Dan had a job. It was The Crochet Crowd or bust. We were all in.

We attended trade shows and experienced one rejection after another. We knew we were onto something, though, and that something was that a lot of education was going to take place online. And that included

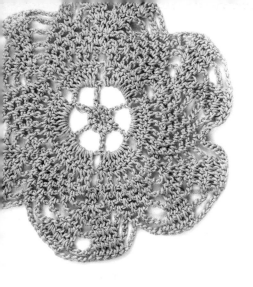

crocheting. We wanted to prove the power of outreach through social media and we had the statistics to back this up. Traditional marketing was the bucket that was falling down the hill with Jack and Jill.

We licked our wounds and learned one lesson after another. In 2012, we decided to attend yet another Craft and Hobby Association Trade Show, and that is where we got our first break. It's the show where we met the yarn company Red Heart, which led us to work with them in 2013. We also ended up winning best *'On The Rise YouTube Channel'* that year, which meant 24 hours of being featured on the home page of *YouTube* itself. It was a breakthrough moment.

In 2013, we started with Red Heart educational tutorials and it gave us perspective on the realm and size of the stitching world. That same year, we hit 100,000 followers on *Facebook* and 50 million views on *YouTube*. We also started planning our first Crochet Cruises and did newsletters, combining tutorial videos with text tips. We also started the stitch-alongs (also known as crochet-alongs) that year. In 2014, we also won *YouTube's* Silver Play award. The community was building.

Our next big, big break came with Spinrite. It just so happened they had a store 30 minutes from our Ontario home. I would buy yarn, teach classes there, and exchange gossip with learners and staff. (Thank gawd the yarn balls didn't tie themselves into a knot.) For several years, we did tent sale ball blowouts. Honestly, a store visit was a highlight of any day. It put us in touch with real people.

In doing social media promotions for our store visits, we knew the store was directly affected by an increase in attendance, and it was no surprise that it grabbed the attention of Spinrite corporate. I knew my analytics cold (it is my morning read with a cup of tea), which led to us working directly with Spinrite in 2015.

The relationship with Spinrite had allowed us to see things in a different way. It was literally like a yarn fairy godmother had waved her magic wand and transformed what we couldn't see as a small business. It was almost blinding but so incredible that we couldn't look away.

Today, we have 1.3 million followers on *Facebook* and a million followers on *YouTube*. Our videos have been viewed almost 185 million times. In the process, we have created one of the largest crochet video libraries in the world.

It has been a journey. One we are still on. It has always been about the community and it still is. It is about the stories we share when yarn brings us together. We are here for the love of the yarn. Community isn't just a buzzword, it's the fibre that drives everything we do.

"Inspire, Create and Celebrate."

Building A Community One Stitch at a Time

When Grace McGrath retired from her career as a federal civil servant in 2018, she decided to set out on her own on a road trip from her home in Henderson, Nevada. Her ultimate goal was to attend her 50th high school reunion on the other side of the country, in Troy, New York. The trip would take two months. As she travelled through large and small communities, she would stop for the night on a whim, posting her adventures of the day on *Facebook*.

By day three, something began happening. Members of The Crochet Crowd community, many of whom she has met on the Crochet Cruises, began noticing her posts. "I was contacted almost every single day to see if we could meet along the way," she says. "My crochet friends started offering to host me overnight which I graciously accepted. I would never dream of imposing on anyone or inviting myself anywhere."

She made stops in California, Arizona, Georgia, Florida, Michigan, Virginia, North Carolina and Pennsylvania to meet up with Crochet Crowd friends. One travelled from Maine to rendezvous with her in Boston. In Oakboro, North Carolina, Crochet Crowd member Teri Hathcock not only offered her a place to stay but invited other crochet friends over for a potluck. Over the 11,000-mile journey Grace met up with nearly 100 different family, friends and Crochet Crowd members. Some offered her an overnight stay while others met for lunch or a quick cup of coffee.

Belonging

"Being a part of The Crochet Crowd has changed my life," says Grace. "It has made me a better person, a better friend and more outgoing."

The Crochet Crowd is about community–a community of people that includes Ann Feist of Mankato, Minnesota, who spent weeks thumbing through each category on our site, looking for broken links. It is people like Bernice Bacon of Lexington, Georgia, who performed a little intervention on me in year two of our cruises to remind me that it's okay to take time out for myself and away from the community. Whenever I'm overwhelmed, I think of her.

The Crochet Community extends far beyond the borders of North America. Geeta Khanna lives in Mumbai, India, where she crochets incredibly intricate dresses and other projects. Debbie Pickering from Tasmania joined us on a cruise where she crocheted a frog she had created from scratch. Then she took the frog on a trip around the United States, taking its picture at stops along the way.

Rosita Ruiz de Chavez lives just outside of Mexico City. She's been teaching her 12-year-old grandson Abel to crochet by doing the Llama which is a tough project.

Cathie Jones and her daughter Amanda were looking for a pattern for a hat when they stumbled across a *YouTube* video of none other than me teaching a tutorial on the subject. It was sometime around 2013 and Jones says she was drawn to our approach, crocheting while I teach a lesson, chatting about everything and anything. Cathie, who hails from Toronto, Ontario, is known for making up songs and singing them on the fly without warning.

"There are many reasons we follow The Crochet Crowd," she says. "Beyond all else, it's the camaraderie and friendships that we have established with many people from around the world, as well as our friendship over the years with Michael and Daniel."

Jones learned to crochet watching her mother and grandmother when she was six years old, but she admits that she never developed the patience that other women in her family show for working on intricate patterns and details.

The first project Cathie tackled with The Crochet Crowd was an afghan of 20 squares. As she worked on the pattern she learned how to do treble stitches, doubles, half doubles, and so much more, including how to braid the squares together.

"The Crochet Crowd has taught me so much and I have a stronger sense for crochet since becoming a member. It has personally challenged me to become a part of a group that forces me to read and follow patterns."

Without the encouragement of other members and being able to see their posts about their own crochet challenges, I wouldn't have succeeded the way that I have. We have developed many wonderful friendships in the group over the last few years.

In the end The Crochet Crowd is about more than just the art of crochet. It's about belonging. It's about the amazing, interesting and creative people we have met over the years, and who support us and our wacky ways. We are very grateful that some of them agreed to participate in this book and share their wonderful creations.

Our community is our extended family. It is huge and growing larger every day. Each member of The Crochet Crowd informs our work, offering an enormous source of ideas and inspiration.

In the end The Crochet Crowd is about more than just the art of crochet. It's about belonging. It's about the amazing, interesting and creative people we have met over the years, and who support us and our wacky ways.

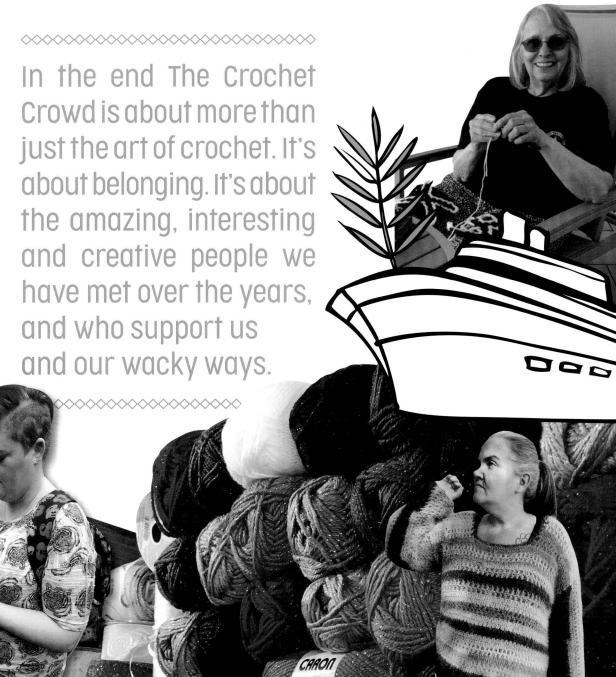

Success

Moving here was the best decision we ever made.

Moving to Nova Scotia

Our journey didn't start here in Nova Scotia, on Canada's east coast, but it was definitely a new beginning in our lives. It wasn't anything scientific, but we chose to live close to the small town of Wolfville, Nova Scotia, home of Acadia University and in the heart of Nova Scotia's fertile Annapolis Valley. Truthfully, Daniel was looking for a different climate to expand his gardening opportunities.

Nova Scotia is a special place. Thrust out into the Atlantic Ocean it is nearly an island, save for a narrow piece of land that connects it to the neighbouring province of New Brunswick. On one side of us is the North Atlantic; on the other side the Bay of Fundy churns out the highest tides in the world – high enough to cover a five-storey building. The amount of water that flows out of the bay twice every day is greater than the outflow of every river in the world combined.

Nova Scotia is larger than the state of New York but has a population the size of Austin, Texas.

The Valley, as it's known, is almost 8,400 square kilometres (3,200 square miles) in area – about three times the size of Rhode Island. It's one of the great agricultural centres of Canada – a place famous for developing and producing new varieties of apples and award-winning wines.

It's a gorgeous region, with red rocky shores and powerful tides, salt marshes, sandy beaches and the ever-changing patchwork of fields, orchards and vineyards.

The summers are warm and fragrant. And the winters can be snowy and picture-postcardy. At harvest time in the fall, there's nothing better than slipping on a cozy sweater and visiting the farm market stands amid the riot of nature's colours and smells.

Everywhere you go here, there are vegetable farms, apple orchards, vineyards. You can watch cattle grazing in a field. In late summer, you can buy locally grown cantaloupes and watermelon. There's even a luffa farmer (yes, the scrubby stuff you use in the shower.) And Wolfville, the town where we live nearby, is a beautiful, bustling little place, with about 4,200 year-round residents and 3,800 students at Acadia University.

With all that great soil, Daniel can indulge his passion for digging in the dirt and gettin' jiggy with the junipers. Oh. And there's an amazing

Patchwork

The Gaspereau Valley is a microcosm of agricultural activity tucked into a deep, narrow valley just a mile or so wide. Patchwork farms straddle both sides of the Gaspereau River growing everything from market vegetables, to apples and corn, and there is all manner of livestock. Every spring, small fish also called Gaspereau by the locals, make their way up the river to spawn and are sometimes caught in nets during their runs.

The Gaspereau Valley lies just a few miles south of where we live, nestled inside a cleft in the South Mountain. Near the valley floor a flock of Cotswold sheep graze among the more common Lincoln and Dorset varieties. The wool of this endangered heritage breed eventually becomes a part of our art.

Gaspereau Valley Fibres sells its own Cotswold wool along with many other Canadian, organic and local natural and hand-painted yarns. The store has amazing yarns, not only from their own sheep but from a range of independent yarn makers. One of the brands we found there was a limited edition Fleece Artist collection of National Parks. Each colouring was dedicated to a provincial park across Canada. Incredibly rich colours and truly inspirational.

Brenda and her crew are engaged. Bounce an idea off them; they love it. And visiting the farm store is like stepping back in time with a wood stove keeping the joint warm in the winter. It's definitely a place to visit when coming to our region.

> ❖❖❖❖❖❖❖❖❖❖❖❖❖❖❖
>
> ## Visiting the store is like stepping back in time.
>
> ❖❖❖❖❖❖❖❖❖❖❖❖❖❖❖

independent yarn store just a short drive away, in a renovated barn. They also produce wool from their own sheep.

We've got five and a half acres on this property which gives Daniel lots of room to be creative with his man tractor. It's allowed us to spend as much time as we can outside.

The Tide Is High, Except When It's Not

We love watching the changing water levels in the nearby Cornwallis River, especially when it drops almost 23 metres (75 feet).

We're also no more than 30 minutes away from some of the most gorgeous beaches, including our favourite local one, Blue Beach, with its million-year-old fossil cliffs and rocky and red-sand shore.

When we're faced with tight deadlines and crazy projects, we need to find a way to find joy and beauty in simple things. That's why Nova Scotia was the perfect move for us.

We can breathe in the life around us. Watch the birds fly by, listen to the leaves rustle, plunge our hands into the luscious, dark earth of a flower bed, feel the sun on our face or the wind in our hair, dip our toes into the ocean, and take our 100-pound puppy for a walk.

Moving here was the best decision we ever made.

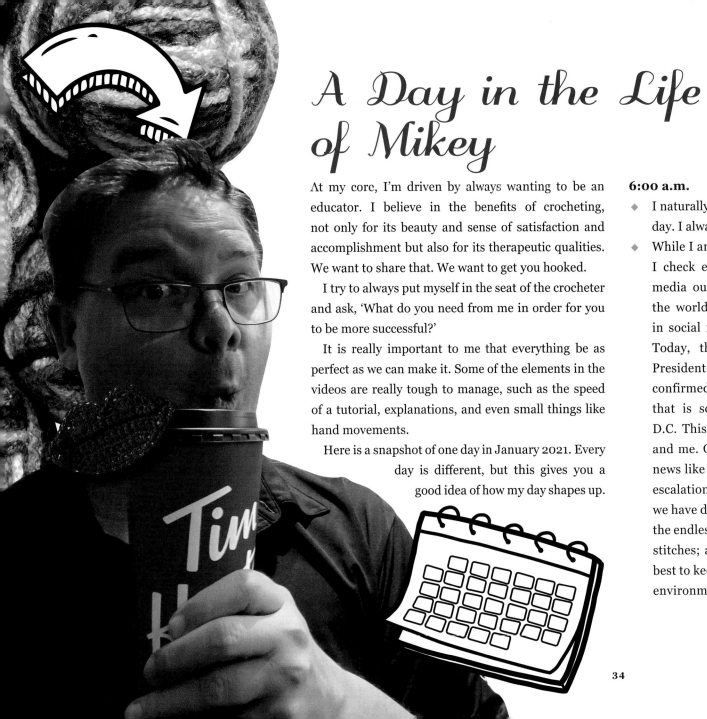

A Day in the Life of Mikey

At my core, I'm driven by always wanting to be an educator. I believe in the benefits of crocheting, not only for its beauty and sense of satisfaction and accomplishment but also for its therapeutic qualities. We want to share that. We want to get you hooked.

I try to always put myself in the seat of the crocheter and ask, 'What do you need from me in order for you to be more successful?'

It is really important to me that everything be as perfect as we can make it. Some of the elements in the videos are really tough to manage, such as the speed of a tutorial, explanations, and even small things like hand movements.

Here is a snapshot of one day in January 2021. Every day is different, but this gives you a good idea of how my day shapes up.

6:00 a.m.

◆ I naturally wake up, rise, shower and dress for the day. I always give the dog a morning treat.

◆ While I am waiting for the Tim Hortons to open, I check email, news and social feeds. I check media outlets, so I know what's happening in the world, and so that if a sly remark is used in social media I have an idea what it's about. Today, there's drama in the United States. President-elect Joe Biden's win is expected to be confirmed, and there is a protest at the Capitol that is scheduled later today in Washington, D.C. This will be a high alert day for my team and me. Our social networks can be affected by news like this. We have to act quickly to prevent escalation should a cyber fight occur. Over years, we have developed guidelines to help us navigate the endless cyber bullying. Some slip through the stitches; as a community, we all have to do our best to keep our social platforms an inspirational environment and safe place to be.

7:00 - 7:20 a.m.

- Order is placed with local Tim Hortons.
- Lift the PuppiDawg into the car and pick up and return with breakfast. Plus, PuppiDawg gets a Timbit if she is noticed!

7:20 - 8:00 a.m.

- I work from home with a dedicated office set up and have breakfast at my desk.
- I check our analytics and see how our new web posts are doing. I also see what past articles are getting attention. This is critical to the next part of my day. If things are falling, I find answers and resolve issues in real time.
- I check on the health and statistical data for *YouTube* for the past video and run an analytics overview on where the video is and overall impressions by the community.
- The *Facebook* Story needs to be created to run 24 hours. I have to decide the story based on what I see bubbling up from the past day and decide whether to give a pattern or concept another 24-hour spin-cycle in social media.
- I have answered all of the outstanding questions on the blog comments to clear me for the day.

8:00 - 11:00 a.m.

- Spring Stitch Along for March 2021 arrived last night.
- Locate this spring's introduction music for the stitch along. Surf a service we use to listen to clips and find the vibe to match the project. I'm looking for high energy with a toe-tapping beat.
- Print out and scan the Stitch Along pattern. There are nine pages and I am scanning for possible errors plus I am going to do swatch samples. Collect my yarn and if I have any questions, I need to contact Yarnspirations. Mentally, I am putting together a storyboard to follow. I have been given two weeks to complete the task. I am suspecting 10 solid days for this. Stress levels increase to hit the deadlines.
- Create a new filing index for the new stitch along and carry through resources from past Stitch Alongs, such as graphics.
- Form a list of questions, such as timelines, requests for graphics, and how much detail I can share in introductions. Emails fired off.

11:00 - 11:30 a.m.

- Write a pattern and match together resources.
- Today, my Loom Knit Wrap went out. Photography was done two days ago. Hours later, there doesn't seem to be much interest in the pattern. However, there's a lot going on in the world today, so I have to figure out if it's the project or world issues. Will this pattern be a bust? I can only tell really in about seven days from now. Time will tell.

11:30 - 12:30 p.m.

- My team (I affectionately call them "the girls") is talking about Valentine's concepts and new patterns. The girls are chatting among themselves throughout the morning about concepts and community issues. Today it includes *Facebook* programming and algorithmic concepts. Wendy located some new patterns that came out that have visual interest.
- A complaint has arrived via email regarding *Facebook* programming behaviour. This is beyond our scope but the crocheter wants an explanation. The girls will know if anything is changing on *Facebook*. I have deferred this to the girls to resolve. This is now on the to-do list to follow up on later today. There are communications bouncing back and forth. I'm letting the team do its magic behind the scenes.

12:30 - 1:00 p.m.

- Feedback from the Stitch Along has come back.
- Some of the questions have been answered but some resources aren't ready for me to start filming yet. I can start organizing and creating some of the Stitch Along samples that need to be done prior to filming which I will begin this evening. Eighteen square motifs are to be done ASAP to begin.
- Plan a photoshoot here with the yarn of choice as backup, non-studio, photos.
- Go through the pattern and label balls with letters so I will not get confused.

LUNCH:

Lunch usually comes courtesy of Daniel who loves to make us a hot meal. Kraft Dinner is on days when I am really upset. It's comfort food.

AFTERNOON:

Today I am writing out patterns and working with my team again. Also conference calls with Yarnspirations, discussions about web security and strategy, and a break to clear our heads and take PuppiDawg for a walk.

5:00 p.m.

- The office usually winds down around five o'clock, and we try to take time to prepare food, wash dishes, and get back into the real world. The pets will be fed after I am done with the dishes and the counters are cleaned and ready to go.

6:30 p.m.

- Final clean-up of the kitchen before I announce, "The kitchen is closed for the night!" My mom used to say that, and I've carried that tradition forward.

7:00 p.m.

- It's time to start preparing the night's crochet project(s). I am starting to make the 18 squares for the Stitch Along. Crocheting is not work for me and before I know it, it is 11 p.m. and time for bed.

11:20 p.m.

- Goodnight. See you tomorrow.

"The Crowd is home to me."

Hooking on the High Seas

Our first personal cruise experience wasn't our best one. We were virgins trying a new adventure on our own. For one thing, I left my crochet at home! Who would do that? I went a little stir crazy while on board. I needed something to occupy my time and I didn't know what to do with myself.

My other issue is that I LOVE my Coca-Cola. I thought the drinks were included. They weren't. It was $2.75 for a glass of Coke, and I found out about the drinks package a little too late.

Being on a a ship of 5,000 people was lonely as hell. I was imagining crocheting and enjoying the gossip with other crocheters AND of course the dessert buffet right next to us.

I vowed the next time we went on a cruise that we would be with people we know. That was the beginning of an idea! When we got home, I asked our cruise agent how to book a group. And that's how the Crochet Cruises got started.

Since then, it has been an amazing crochet party on the high seas.

With The Crochet Crowd spread around the world, it was important for us to find ways to connect with our new friends — not just over the Internet but in person too. Crochet Cruises seemed perfect for that.

We've done a lot of live, in-person shows over the years and they've always been popular with The Crochet Crowd. But our cruises take that connection to the next level. They allow us to get to know everyone much more than we ever could do at one of our shows, and we've found that people like spending more time with us than just a two-hour workshop. It's a way to meet friends, learn the art of crochet, and have a really good time doing it.

Our inaugural sailing took place in February 2014. We travelled to the Eastern Caribbean and the Mexican Riviera. The first two cruises were a hit and as soon as the adventure ended we immediately began taking bookings for the next year. Since then we've tried to do two or three cruises a year.

We usually get about 100 participants. About 60 of them come back for more. On a seven-day cruise, we host five to seven workshops, in addition to other fun activities — activities designed to make sure

#YARNSPIRATIONS

everybody gets to know each other. Many people say they've made lifelong friends.

We set a theme a few months before we set sail and ask everybody to have their pieces of "homework" ready by the time they get to the ship. We encourage people to exchange their squares with others to create a true community blanket. Once the exchange happens, we supply the yarn so people can finish their blankets.

After we assemble our group projects, we donate them to an organization, or cruisers take them home to donate in their own communities.

On our 2017 cruises to the Caribbean each of our cruisers crocheted four squares for an afghan to create 266 blankets to donate to first responders. Every year we've done something similar.

The cruises and retreats are an amazing experience, especially for me. I'm exhausted but energized at the end of the trip. We have laughed together, cried together, and celebrated the wonderful world of crochet together.

The two Caribbean cruises we have planned for 2022 will be the last ones under the format we've been using since 2014. Evolution is key and we are moving onto something new.

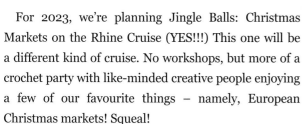

For 2023, we're planning Jingle Balls: Christmas Markets on the Rhine Cruise (YES!!!) This one will be a different kind of cruise. No workshops, but more of a crochet party with like-minded creative people enjoying a few of our favourite things – namely, European Christmas markets! Squeal!

Because we've had such a blast hookin' the high seas, we've included some photos from those trips in this book. We can't wait for 2022!

CROCHET CRUISES

Here's where we've been with our high-seas hookers!

2014: Two cruises — Eastern Caribbean and Mexican Riviera

2015: Two cruises —Eastern and Western Caribbean

2016: Three cruises Western and Eastern Caribbean as well as Alaska

2017: Three cruises — Hawaii and Eastern and Western Caribbean

2018: Two cruises: Southern Caribbean and Alaska

2019: Two cruises Mardi Gras – New Orleans and Panama Canal

2020: Southeastern Caribbean

Patterns

One of the greatest joys of running with The Crochet Crowd is to witness the unbelievable talent and inventiveness of our community. We see it every day, and we see it around the world. Talking and interacting with the community of "The Crowd" is home to me. If it weren't for the internet, all of the friendships we have would not have happened.

Watching our community learn and grow is the most wonderful thing about belonging to The Crochet Crowd. Many of our community's patterns have received recognition throughout the crochet community and we couldn't be prouder.

Daniel and I, of course, have contributed patterns to this book. What we are really excited about though, is introducing to you some yarn enthusiasts of our community. As you will see, their skill and their pieces reflect the diversity of The Crochet Crowd. They are quite simply — beautiful.

We have scarves and cowls, baby blankets, headbands, wraps and hats. We also have a bonus afghan by Jeanne Steinhilber that is simply stunning. Come on along and meet everybody!

All patterns in this book are in North American (US) terms.

Disclaimer: We tried our very best to be error free and it's possible that some mistakes may have fallen between the stitches. Please let us know and we can make changes for later printing releases.

Meet And Greet

I love crochet and I love being an educator. If I am not crocheting, I am thinking about it. I don't like to be bored so I like challenges and try patterns only once.

I promise you won't be bored here.

Here are my fellow designers. You will be glad you met them.

Daniel Zondervan

Daniel's patterns demonstrate his incredible eye for colour and design.

He graduated from Wilfrid Laurier University in Waterloo with a degree in music with a major in performance music. After graduation, he started organizing baroque music concerts, eventually forming Nota Bene Period

Orchestra, with Daniel playing viola and viola da gamba. Nota Bene is still going strong today.

Daniel has worked as a choir director and organist for local churches, and has conducted vocal and handbell choirs. When we met in Walkerton, he was rediscovering his passion for landscaping and garden design.

Whatever the medium, Daniel must be creative. It feeds his soul. He always pushes us to use our imagination to design beyond boundaries.

Anita Grover

On our first Alaskan Cruise, a last-minute reservation request came in from a woman named Anita Grover. We found room for her to join us and we are glad we did! Her energy and smile are contagious.

Anita is hooked on Tunisian Crochet and Dela Wilkins was our Tunisian expert and guest teacher for the trip.

Anita started her crochet journey when her youngest son wanted her to make him a red and blue striped hat with a matching scarf. He wanted it *made with love*, code for handmade. She said she didn't know how but her son literally wouldn't let her off the hook. Give *YouTube* a try, he told her and she found The Crochet Crowd.

Her outlook on life inspires me to keep calm and crochet on. When the ship gets rocky, Anita's smile brings smooth sailing ahead. When there is an opportunity to help others, she is always there.

We are delighted to reveal some extraordinary design skills from one of the nicest people you'll meet.

Jeanne Steinhilber

Jeanne has been crocheting for 50 years. She is propelled by the joy that creativity brings and is adept at all kinds of arts and crafts, from pastel drawings to scrapbooking and photography.

Her first memory is learning to crochet from her mom to earn a Girl Scout badge. In her twenties, she loved to make and gift baby blankets for her family and friends.

Jeanne thrives on reading patterns and loves a challenging design, pulling out tips and tricks to build her personal toolbox of stitches that she will inevitably incorporate into future projects.

The Ribbed Glacier Cowl was her first of many viral patterns but her breakthrough design came with a blanket that she created for her granddaughter. Called *Hugs & Kisses Baby Blanket*, it features cross stitches and bobbles, like hugs and kisses represented by Xs and Os. It was inspired by the Stitch is Right game where online crocheters would spin the virtual wheels to find out their next colour, row counts, and stitch to be used.

Like the structure in her life, the Hugs and Kisses concept is methodical, thoughtful and visual eye candy. This pattern has been downloaded nearly 200,000 times!

Kathleen Neborak Nolen

We met Kathy in 2015 at the Spinrite Tent Sale in North Carolina and she booked the following year's Crochet Cruise with us. Kathy learned to crochet from her mother and grandmother when she was a young girl. She learned more stitches and continued into adulthood with crochet as her hobby.

Kathy is a veteran of the United States Army and she has taken her crochet with her as she was deployed around the world. After 10 years of active duty, she became an Army civilian employee for almost 30 years.

She spent the last 18 years in the Virginia area where she discovered the excitement and curiosity of craft fairs. She was so inspired that she decided to try creating and selling her work.

She understood the importance of researching the right shows to display her projects, starting locally in schools and churches to receive feedback and watch consumer behaviour. What didn't sell in one show was carried forward, building inventory. The next step was to enter juried craft shows. Eventually, she started her own business called Yarn Chef Creations. Over the years, she's developed a clientele and continues to keep her finger on the pulse of the industry.

We are proud to showcase one of her designs here.

Megan McHugh

Like many creative people, Megan learned multiple crafts at an early age. She jokes that she most likely inherited every possible crafting gene in the family. Role models in her life include her Aunt Mary and grandmother.

Crochet was put on the back burner for a while as she explored other fabric arts, including weaving, spinning, sewing and quilting.

We crossed paths years ago when we were hosting one of our Crochet Cruises. Megan and her husband, Bruce, joined us on board and we hooked the high seas together. Bruce dove into the yarn arts, too.

Through members of The Crochet Crowd, Megan found that the world of crochet had changed substantially since the days of the infamous granny square ponchos of 1972 that she and her sister worked on (and never completed), and she became re-hooked on crochet. We are so glad she rediscovered us and that we can share her talents with you.

Study of the Journey

In the belief that everything happens for a reason — the good, the bad and the ugly — the *Study of the Journey* goes beyond visual for me. I wanted to be more metaphoric in my approach to the stitches, binding together and forming pathways. From one stitch to another, life's journey can appear to be random but somehow it is connected from one moment to another.

My mother would come to understand the way I needed to learn, and she used crafts as the trigger for imaginative skill-building for something tangible. In this afghan, the stories and lessons of my journey weave in and out, finding me one day as a trucker and using snail mail to reach out with pen pals, only to discover that life's calling could be a cyber click away.

The *Study of the Journey* blanket is a compilation of skills that I have learned and demonstrated along the way, hopefully bringing them together for a cohesive assembly of lessons blending into one. Of course, some skills in this blanket are new because life never stands still and I believe we are on a continuous journey throughout our lives.

Afghans like this one can take up to 170 hours to design and develop. A lot of testing, frogging, mapping and writing as I go. Sometimes an idea works, other times it doesn't. A stitch that I thought looked decent can really pop out as I continue. I design by starting at the beginning and then examine what could go next. Like life, I use it as an opportunity to take chances and use past lessons to morph the project forward.

Life is too short not to continue to learn, and part of my addiction with crochet is knowing there is something, always something, exciting around the corner, a skill I'll use another day. Happiness to me is in self-discovery. It adds to my capabilities and I push myself to develop skills that maybe others find insignificant. In the end, it's part of my journey and I like you, am unique. Our paths may cross where we share a moment of time when we converge but then end up walking down a different path, wherever that may lead.

Here is to that journey! Here is to your journey.

TO THE JOURNEY
Design by Michael Sellick

Industry professional Sara Arblaster told me crochet is about the "stitching journey." And it truly is. The journey is about the stitches we loved from the past and new stitches we pick up along the way.

The large circular centre of this piece lends itself to easy repeat and memorization, like the increments of a clock. Designing this was a huge challenge for me with lots of math, frogging, and more. But once I got the circle to sit flat, I found myself giggling with delight. You will too!

Materials

Patons® Inspired™ (150 g/5.3 oz, 203 m/222 yds)
Contrast A Silver Gray Heather 4 Balls
Contrast B Pacific Blue 4 Balls
Contrast C Sapphire Teal 3 Balls

Use size 6.5 mm, U.S. K/10.5 hook or hook size to obtain gauge. The project total is 1547 m/1692 yds. You will have some yarn leftover on the last ball of each colour assigned. Measurements approx 60" x 60" [152.5 x 152.5 cm]. Gauge 12 sc and 13 rows = 4" [10 cm].

Special Stitches: The popcorn and shell stitches can be defined many ways. For this pattern it is as follows:

Popcorn = 4 dc in same st, remove hook. Insert hook from front in the top of the first dc in the group of 4. Put loop on hook and pull through first dc st.

Shell = 7 dc in same st.

NOTES

- Join stated at the end of the rounds is assumed to slip stitch to the beginning stitch or top of the beginning chain. Unless otherwise stated.
- For the instructions in rounds, each instruction is followed by a breakdown of stitches and total round. An example at the end of:
  ◊ Round 14: Join. Break. 16 groups of 7 dtr, 16 sc and 32 ch 1 sps. 160 sts. It has the number of grouped stitches such as 16 in this case. With the count of 16 single crochet and 32 ch 1 spaces. Followed at the end for a total stitch count for the entire round.
- Here are the instructions for the blanket transitioning from the circle to a square. It will give the total stitch count per side and then a total stitch count for the entire round. An example is the end of:
  ◊ Round 44: Join with hdc. 125 sts. 500 sts. There are 125 stitches per side and 500 stitches around.

Where It All Began

1st rnd: (RS) With A, ch 3 (ch 3 doesn't count as st in this rnd). 12 dc in 3rd ch from hook. Join with sl st to top of first dc. 12 dc.

2nd rnd: Ch 1, 2 sc in same sp as sl st. 2 sc in each st around. Join. 24 sc.

3rd rnd: Ch 1, 1 sc in same sp as sl st. 1 sc next st, ch 2, sk next st. *1 sc in next 2 sts, ch 2, sk next st. Rep from * around. Join. Break. 16 sc and 8 ch 2 sps.

4th rnd: With C, join with sl st to next ch 2 sp. Ch 3 (counts as dc in this round and throughout). 4 dc in same ch 2 sp. *5 dc in next ch 2 sp. Rep from * around. Join. Break. 40 dc.

TIP: In the next round, our testers thought it would be easier for you to put a stitch marker at the top of trfp. It's easier to find where the 2 sc goes into the top of the trfp in rnd 6.

5th rnd: With B, join with standing sc in the same sl st. 1 sc in next 4 st. 1 trfp around both sc sts in 3rd rnd. The trfp is an extra st that is in front to help the circle grow bigger. Start next st in the next group of 5 sts. *1 sc in next 5 sts, 1 trfp around both sc sts in 3rd rnd. Rep from * around. Join. 40 sc and 8 trfp.

6th rnd: Ch 1, *1 dcfp around the last trfp st that we just passed in rnd 5. 1 sc in next st, ch 2, sk next st, 1 sc in next st, 1 dcfp around next trfp in rnd 5, 2 sc in top of trfp st. Rep from * around. Join to beg dcfp. Break. 8 ch 2 sps, 32 sc and 16 dcfp.

Crocheted by Wendy Marple

Caron® Cotton Cakes™ (250 g/8.8 oz, 485 m/530 yds)
Contrast A White 2 balls
Contrast B Frosted Pink 2 balls
Contrast C Aqua Breeze 1 Ball
  Use size 5 mm, U.S. H/8. Measurements 44" square [112 cm square].

Crocheted by Nancy Elliot

Scheepjes® Colour Crafter™ (100 g/3.5 oz, 300 meters/328 yards)
Contrast A Pollare 2 Balls
Contrast B Texel 1 Ball
Contrast C Oostende 1 Ball
Contrast D Middleburg 1 Ball
Contrast E The Hague 1 Ball
Contrast F Zandvoort 1 Ball
Contrast G Enschede 1 Ball
  Use size 4 mm, U.S. G/6 hook or size to obtain gauge.DK Yarn Weight, #3 weight U.S. Gauge after 7 rounds, it should measure approx. 4" [10 cm] dia. Measurements approx 42.5" square [108 cm].

7th rnd: With A, standing sc in same sp as sl st. 1 sc in next st. 2 sc in ch 2 sp. *1 sc in next 6 sts, 2 sc in next ch 2 sp. Rep from * around to last 4 sts. 1 sc in last 4 sts. Join. 64 sc.

8th rnd: Ch 6 (counts as dc and ch 3 sp). 1 dc in next st. *Sk 2 sts, 1 dc in next st, ch 3, 1 dc in next st. - big v-stitch made. Rep from * around. Join to 3rd ch of beg ch 6. Break. 16 big v-sts.

9th rnd: With C, join with sl st to next ch 3 sp. Ch 1, (1 sc, 1 hdc, 1 dc, ch 1, 1 dc, 1 hdc, 1 sc, ch 1) in same ch 3 sp. *(1 sc, 1 hdc, 1 dc, ch 1, 1 dc, 1 hdc, 1 sc, ch 1) in next ch 3 sp. Rep from * around. Join. Break. 32 sc, 32 hdc, 32 dc and 16 ch 1 sps.

10th rnd: With A with standing sc in ch 1 sp of the next petal point. Ch 5, *1 sc in next ch 1 on the next petal. Ch 5. Rep from * around. Join. 16 ch 5 sps and 16 sc.

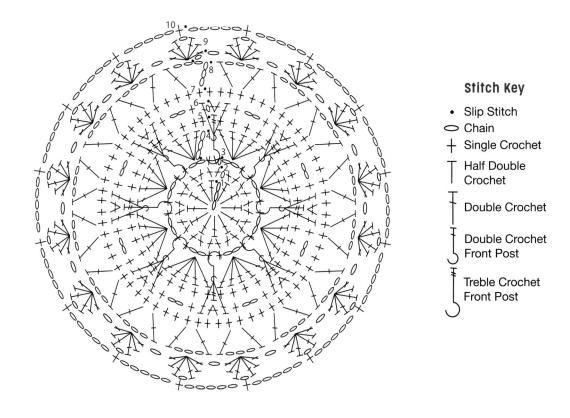

Stitch Key

- • Slip Stitch
- ⌒ Chain
- ┼ Single Crochet
- ┬ Half Double Crochet
- ┬ Double Crochet
- ┬ Double Crochet Front Post
- ┬ Treble Crochet Front Post

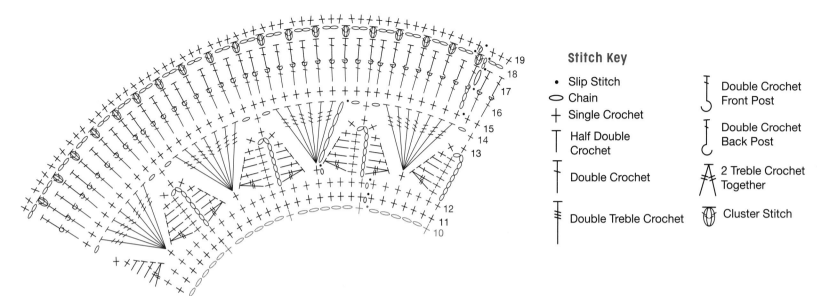

Stitch Key

- Slip Stitch
- Chain
- Single Crochet
- Half Double Crochet
- Double Crochet
- Double Treble Crochet

- Double Crochet Front Post
- Double Crochet Back Post
- 2 Treble Crochet Together
- Cluster Stitch

Sunshine Rays Section

11th rnd: Continue with A, ch 1, 1 sc in same join sp. 6 sc in next ch 5 sp, *1 sc in next sc st. 6 sc in next ch 5 sp. Rep from * around. Join. 112 sc.

The next rnd is the foundation of building the sunshine rays.

12th rnd: Ch 1, 1 sc in same join sp. Ch 8. 1 sc in 3rd ch from hook, 1 sc in next 5 chs. 1 sc in next 6 sts, *1 sc in next st, ch 8, 1 sc 3rd ch from hook, 1 sc in next 5 chs, 1 sc in next 6 sts. Rep from * around. Join. Break. 112 sc and 16 ch petals.

13th rnd: With B, join with sl st to middle sc between two ch petals. Ch 1, 1 sc in same join sp. *Sk to the 4th st to begin using only the ch petals, tr2tog using

next 2 sts, 1 dc in next st, 1 hdc in next 2 sts, 1 sc in next st, 3 sc in ch sp at the tip of petal. 1 sc in next st, 1 hdc in next 2 sts, 1 dc in next st, tr2tog using next 2 sts. **1 sc in 4th st between the ch petals. Rep from * around to the start of last petal. Rep * to ** once. Join. Break. 16 petals around. 13 sts per petal, 1 sc between each petal. 224 sts.

The project will appear to buckle, but keep on going.

14th rnd: With A, join with sl st to same join sp. Ch 5 (counts as dtr), 6 dtr in same join sp. Ch 1, 1 sc in the middle sc of the next petal point. Ch 1. *7 dtr in next sc between petals, ch 1, 1 sc in the middle sc of the next petal point, ch 1. Rep from * around. Join. Break. 16 groups of 7 dtr, 16 sc and 32 ch 1 sps. 160 sts.

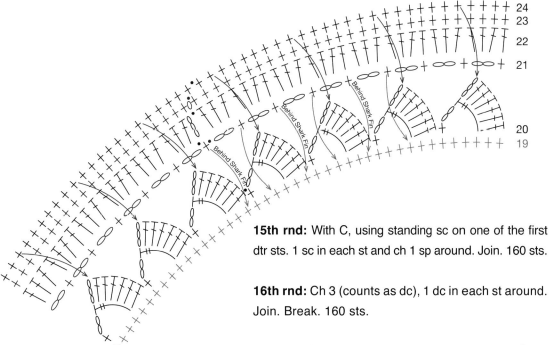

Numbers on the chart: 24, 23, 22, 21, 20, 19

Labels on chart: Behind Shark Fin, Behind Shark Fin, Behind Shark Fin, Behind Shark Fin

Stitch Key

- • Slip Stitch
- ⬭ Chain
- + Single Crochet
- ⊤ Double Crochet
- ⊤ Treble Crochet
- ↘ Arrow indicates where stitch is placed.

15th rnd: With C, using standing sc on one of the first dtr sts. 1 sc in each st and ch 1 sp around. Join. 160 sts.

16th rnd: Ch 3 (counts as dc), 1 dc in each st around. Join. Break. 160 sts.

17th rnd: With A, join with sl st to same join sp. Ch 1, 1 dcfp around same post as join, 1 dcbp around next st. *1 dcfp around next st, 1 dcbp around next st. Rep from * around. Join. Break. 160 sts.

18th rnd: With B, join with sl st to same join sp. Ch 2, cluster in the same sp as join. Ch 2. *Sk next st, cluster in next st, ch 2. Rep from * around. Join. Break. 80 clusters and 80 ch 2 sps.

19th rnd: With A, join with sl st to next ch 2 sp. Ch 1, *3 sc in each ch 2 sp around. Break. Turn. 240 sc.

Around the Mulberry Bush Section

The next round, we need to work on the WS (Wrong Side). We are going to create shark fins, but we want them to lean back into the project; so it must be completed on the wrong side. There are multiple steps to make one fin.

20th rnd: WS With C, join with standing sc to same join sp. Starting in the same stitch as join. Shark fin st around. Join. Break. Turn. 40 shark fins.

21st rnd: RS Lean fins forward toward you and work behind fins. With B, join with standing sc in next st in rnd 19. Ch 2, sk 2 sts on 19th rnd which includes the st that the shark fin uses, 1 sc in next st. Sk next 2 sts, ch 2. *1 sc in next st on 19th rnd, ch 2, sk 2 sts on 19th rnd. Rep from * around. Join. 80 ch 2 sp and 80 sc.

TIP: Read carefully the next rnd.

22nd rnd: Sl st to next ch 2 sp. Ch 3 (counts as dc), 2 dc in same sp. 3 dc in next ch 2 sp, 1 dc in next sc st. *3 dc in next 2 ch 2 sps, 1 dc in next sc. Rep from * around. Join. 280 dc.

23rd rnd: Ch 1, 1 sc in each st around. Join. Break. 280 sc.

24th rnd: With A, join with standing sc 1 st before the

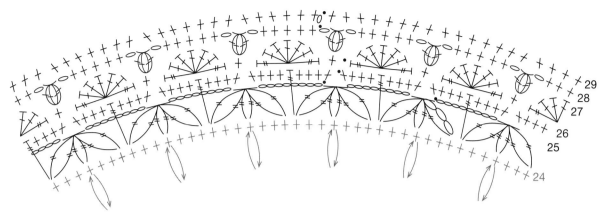

Stitch Key

•	Slip Stitch
⬭	Chain
+	Single Crochet
†	Double Crochet
‡	Treble Crochet
	Beginning Sunset Reflection Stitch
	Sunset Reflection Stitch
	Popcorn Stitch

join, 1 sc in next 4 sts, 1 sc in next st going through the space between the ch 3 and n9c post of the first shark fin to pin it back. *1 sc in next 6 sts, 1 sc going through shark fin post first and next st together. Rep from * around. 1 sc in last 2 sts. Join. 280 sc.

Sunsets Section

The Sunset Reflection Stitch uses 7 stitches for each sunset. It consists of Tr6tog with intentional spacing between the groups. 2 of each of the rays of the sunset share the same stitch.

25th rnd: *Beg sunset reflection st, ch 8. *Sunset reflection st,* ch 8. Start with using next st. Rep from * around. Join. Break. 40 reflection sunset groups.

26th rnd: With C, join with sl st in any ch 8 sp. Ch 1, in each ch 8 space around [4 sc in ch 8 sp, 1 tr in front of ch 8 sp last st used by the last sunset reflection just passed, 4 sc]. Join. Break. 40 groups of 9. 360 sts.

27th rnd: With B, join with standing sc in same join sp. Sk 3 sts, 1 flat petal st in next tr st, sk 4 sts, *1 sc in next st, sk 3 sts, 1 flat petal st in next st (this is the tr st for reference), sk 4 sts. Rep from * around. Join. Break. 40 flat petals, 40 sc. 320 sts.

28th rnd: With A, join with standing sc on the 2nd st of a flat petal. 1 sc in next 4 sts, ch 1, sk next tr, 1 popcorn in next st, ch 1, sk next st. *1 sc in next 5 sts, sk next st, ch 1, 1 popcorn in next st, ch 1, sk next st. Rep from * around. Join. 40 popcorn, 80 ch 1 sps and 200 sc.

29th rnd: Ch 1, 1 sc in same join sp, 1 sc in next 4 st. 1 sc in each sp before and after next popcorn. *1 sc in next 5 sc sts, 1 sc in each sp before and after next popcorn. Rep from * around. Join. Break. 280 sts.

Transition To A New Life

Prepare the next round with stitch markers to locate the corners. Use the first st as the first corner and place a stitch marker. (Starting in next st, count to the 70th st and mark with a stitch marker.) 3 times. The 70th stitch is after the 10th popcorn in first sc by itself after a stitch that has 2 sc in the top of the popcorn.

When counting the stitches per side, don't include the chain spaces that make up the turn of a corner.

30th rnd: With C, join with sl st to same join sp. Ch 4 (counts as tr), 1 tr in same join sp. *1 tr in next **4 sts**, 1 dc in next **7 sts**, 1 hdc in next **7 sts**, 1 sc in next **33 sts**, 1 hdc in next **7 sts**, 1 dc in next **7 sts**, 1 tr in next **4 sts**. ** (2 tr. Ch 2. 2 tr) in next stitch. Rep from * twice more, then * to ** once. 2 tr in same join sp at the beginning. Join with hdc. 73 sts. 292 sts.

31st rnd: Ch 3 (counts as dc), 1 dc in same join sp. *1 dc in next **14 sts**, 1 hdc in next **14 sts**, 1 sc in next **17 sts**, 1 hdc in next **14 sts**, 1 dc in next **14 sts**. ** (2 dc. Ch 2. 2 dc) in next corner sp. Rep from * twice more, then * to ** once. 2 dc in same join sp at the beginning. Ch 2, join. Break. 77 sts. 308 sts.

32nd rnd: With B, join with sl st to ch 2 sp corner. Ch 3 (counts as dc), 1 dc in same join sp. *1 dc in next **10 sts**, 1 hdc in next **10 sts**, 1 sc in next **37 sts**, 1 hdc in next **10 sts**, 1 dc in next **10 sts**. ** (2 dc. Ch 2. 2 dc)

Stitch Key

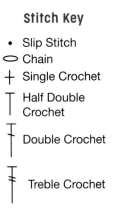

- • Slip Stitch
- ◯ Chain
- + Single Crochet
- ┬ Half Double Crochet
- ┬ Double Crochet
- ‡ Treble Crochet

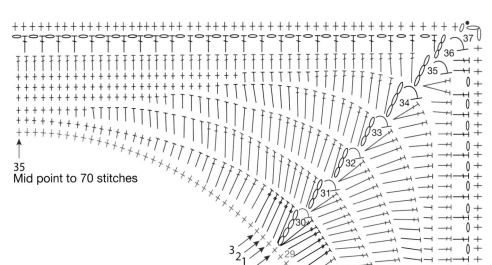

35
Mid point to 70 stitches

37
36
35
34
33
32
31
30
29
280
3 2 1

246 →

---

in next corner sp. Rep from * twice more, then * to ** once. 2 dc in same join sp at the beginning. Join with hdc. 81 sts. 324 sts.

33rd rnd: Ch 3 (counts as dc), 1 dc in same join sp. *1 dc in next **8 sts**, 1 hdc in next **8 sts**, 1 sc in next **49 sts**, 1 hdc in next **8 sts**, 1 dc in next **8 sts.** ** (2 dc. Ch 2. 2 dc) in next corner sp. Rep from * twice more, then * to ** once. 2 dc in same join sp at the beginning. Join with hdc. 85 sts. 340 sts.

34th rnd: Ch 3 (counts as dc), 1 dc in same join sp. *1 dc in next **8 sts**, 1 hdc in next **8 sts**, 1 sc in next **53 sts**, 1 hdc in next 8 sts, 1 dc in next **8 sts.** ** (2 dc. Ch 2. 2 dc) in next corner sp. Rep from * twice more, then * to ** once. 2 dc in same join sp at the beginning. Join with hdc. Break. 89 sts. 356 sts.

35th rnd: With A, join with sl st to ch 2 sp corner. Ch 3 (counts as dc), 1 dc in same join sp. *1 dc in each st to corner. ** (2 dc. Ch 2. 2 dc) in next corner sp. Rep from * twice more, then * to ** once. 2 dc in same join sp at the beginning. Join with hdc. 93 sts. 372 sts.

36th rnd: Ch 3, 1 dc in same corner sp. Ch 1, *sk next st. (1 dc in next st, ch 1, sk next st) 46 times. (2 dc. Ch 2. 2 dc) in next corner sp. Rep from * 2 more times, then * once. 2 dc in beg corner sp. Join with hdc. 97 sts (47 ch 1 sps included). 388 sts

37th rnd: Ch 1, 1 sc in same corner sp. *1 sc in each st and ch 1 sp across. (1 sc. Ch 2. 1 sc) in corner sp. Rep from * 2 more times, then * once. 1 sc in beg corner sp. Ch 2. Join. Break. 99 sts. 396 sts.

Raised Leaves Section

38th rnd: With B, join with sl st to corner sp. Ch 3 (counts as dc), 1 dc in same join sp. *1 dc in each st to corner. ** (2 dc. Ch 2. 2 dc) in next corner sp. Rep from * twice more, then * to ** once. 2 dc in same join sp at the beginning. Join with hdc. 103 sts. 412 sts.

39th rnd: Ch 1 (doesn't count as st), 2 hdc in same sp. 1 dcbp in each st to next corner. ** (2 hdc. Ch 2. 2 hdc) in next corner sp. Rep from * twice more, then * to ** once. 2 hdc in same join sp at the beginning. Ch 2, join. Break. 107 sts. 428 sts.

40th rnd: With C, join with sl st to corner sp. Ch 3, 1 dc in same corner sp. *[Sk next 3 sts. 1 dtrcl in next st. Working behind last dtr, 1 dc in each of 3 skipped sts.] 26 times. Sk next 3 sts, 1 dtrcl in next corner sp, 1 dc in each of the 3 skipped sts.** (1 dc. Ch 2. 2 dc) in next corner sp. Rep from *twice more, then * to ** once. 1 dc in beg corner sp. Join with hdc. 27 arrow sts. 111 sts per side. 444 sts.

41st rnd: Ch 3, 1 dc in same corner sp. *1 dc in next 2 sts. [Sk next st. 1 dc in next 3 sts. Working in front, 1 dtrcl in skipped st.] 27 times. 1 dc in next st.** (2 dc. Ch 2. 2 dc) in corner sp. Rep from * twice more, then * to ** one. 2 dc in beg corner sp. Ch 2, join. Break. 27 arrow sts. 115 sts per side. 460 sts.

42nd rnd: With B, join with sl st to corner sp. Ch 3 (counts as dc), 1 dc in same join sp. *1 dc in each st to corner. ** (2 dc. Ch 2. 2 dc) in next corner sp. Rep from * twice more, then * to ** once. 2 dc in same join sp at the beginning. Join with hdc. 119 sts. 476 sts.

43rd rnd: Ch 1 (doesn't count as st), 2 hdc in same st. 1 dcbp in each st to next corner. ** (2 hdc. Ch 2. 2 hdc) in next corner sp. Rep from * twice more, then * to ** once. 2 hdc in same join sp at the beginning. Ch 2, join. Break. 123 sts. 492 sts.

44th rnd: With A, join with sl st to corner sp. Ch 1, 1 sc in same corner sp. *1 sc in each st across. (1 sc. Ch 2. 1 sc) in corner sp. Rep from * 2 more times, then * once. 1 sc in beg corner sp. Join with hdc. 125 sts. 500 sts.

45th rnd: Ch 3, 1 dc in same corner sp. *Ch 1, sk next st. (1 dc in next st, ch 1, sk next st) 62 times. (2 dc. Ch 2. 2 dc) in next corner sp. Rep from * 2 more times, then * once. 2 dc in beg corner sp. Join with hdc. 63 ch 1 sps per side. 129 sts. 516 sts.

46th rnd: Ch 1, 1 sc in same corner sp. *1 sc in each st and ch 1 sp across. (1 sc. Ch 2. 1 sc) in corner sp. Rep from * 2 more times, then * once. 1 sc in beg corner sp. Ch 2. Join. Break. 131 sts. 524 sts.

Stitch Key

- • Slip Stitch
- ⬭ Chain
- + Single Crochet
- T Half Double Crochet
- ⌐ Half Double Crochet Join
- ⍑ Double Crochet
- ⍑ Double Crochet Back Post
- ⌒ 2 Double Treble Cluster

Note: Dc is behind the 2tr tog as noted in gray.

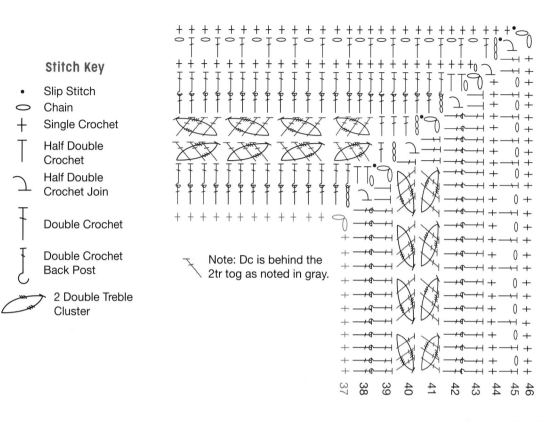

57

Stitch Key

- • Slip Stitch
- ◯ Chain
- + Single Crochet
- ⊤ Half Double Crochet
- ⊤ Double Crochet
- ⤴ Special Together Stitch
- ᗧ Picot

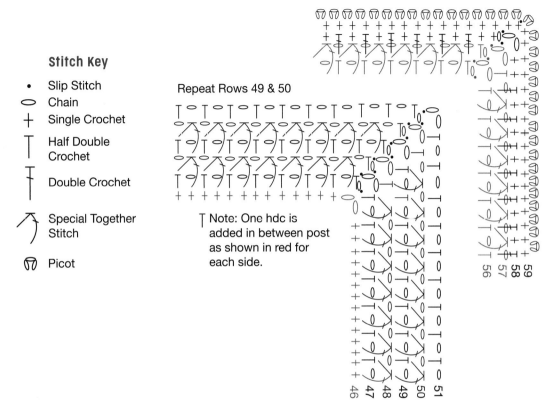

Repeat Rows 49 & 50

⊤ Note: One hdc is added in between post as shown in red for each side.

The Road Less Travelled

As we begin the next round we need to set ourselves up so that the afghan will not buckle in the future. I placed stitch markers after each group of 9 so it's easier to count.

47th rnd: With B, join with sl st to corner sp. Ch 1, 1 hdc in same corner sp. *Ch 1, sk next st. (1 hdc in next

st, ch 1, sk next st) 65 times. (1 hdc. Ch 2. 1 hdc) in next corner sp. Rep from * 2 more times, then * once. 1 hdc in beg corner sp. Ch 2, join. Break. 67 hdc and 66 ch 1 sps per side. 133 sts. 532 sts.

48th rnd: With C, join with sl st to corner sp. Ch 1, 1 hdc in same sp. *[Ch 1, 1 spec tog st]. Rep [ ] to next corner. ** (1 hdc. Ch 2. 1 hdc) in next corner sp. Rep from * 2 more times, then * once. 1 hdc in beg corner sp. Ch 2, join. Break. 66 spec tog sts with 66 ch 1 sps per side and 2 hdc in corner. 134 sts. 536 sts.

TIP: The next rnd for this section has a special added stitch that keeps this section in balance but also helps it to grow outward to stay flat. It's the last stitch before each corner.

49th rnd: With B, join with sl st to corner sp. Ch 1, 1 hdc in same corner sp, *ch 1, sk next st. (1 hdc in next ch 1 sp, ch 1, sk next st) 66 times. 1 hdc between the posts of the spec tog st and last hdc before corner. Ch 1. (1 hdc. Ch 2. 1 hdc) in next corner sp. Rep from * 2 more times, then * once. 1 hdc in beg corner sp. Ch 2, join. Break. 69 hdc sts and 68 ch 1 sps per side. 135 sts. 540 sts.

50th rnd: With A, join with sl st to corner sp. Ch 1, 1 hdc in same sp. *[Ch 1, 1 spec tog st]. Rep to the next corner. ** (1 hdc. Ch 2. 1 hdc) in next corner sp.

Rep from * 2 more times, then * once. 1 hdc in beg corner sp. Ch 2, join. Break. 68 spec tog sts, 68 ch 1 sps, 2 hdc per side. 138 sts. 552 sts.

51st rnd and alt rnds: As rnd 49. Alternate rounds are 53, 55 and 57.

52nd rnd: With C, as rnd 50.
54th rnd: With A, as rnd 50.
56th rnd: With C, as rnd 50.

It's A Wrap - Final Border

58th rnd: With A, join with sl st to corner sp. Ch 1, 1 sc in same corner sp. *1 sc in next hdc, [1 dc in next st 2 rows below, encasing the ch 1 sp in the row below inside st, 1 sc in next st.] Rep [ ] to next corner. (1 sc. Ch 2. 1 sc) in corner sp. Rep from * 2 more times, then * once. 1 sc in beg corner sp. Join with hdc. 76 dc sts and 79 sc sts per side. 155 sts. 620 sts.

59th rnd: Ch 1, 1 sc in same corner sp. Picot, 1 sc in same corner sp. *(1 sc in next st, picot, 1 sc in next st) to next corner. [1 sc in corner, picot, 1 sc in same corner sp.] twice. Rep from * 2 more times, then * once. 1 sc in last corner sp, picot, 1 sc in same sp. Join. Fasten off.

Tidal Bay Series

We've named these three patterns the Tidal Bay Series as a tribute to our home in Nova Scotia. There's a thriving wine industry here and Tidal Bay is the province's first wine appellation. It denotes excellence and wholesome, clean flavour, qualities we hope you'll find in these relatively easy three patterns.

Daniel's pattern is simple and has a fantastic breathing feel that is light and yet texturally awesome to look at. Daniel added a half double crochet to help break up the texture. Plus, he loves the tight stripe look that naturally occurs using Red Heart Unforgettable. Megan enjoyed the stitch combination so much that she decided to work on a Mobius cowl and matching headband. Why? Because the stitch looks amazing on both sides. Reversible and so much fun to make.

Daniel's stitching combination is easy to remember and the stitch is reversible, meaning the stitchwork texture appears on both sides of the project. If you are like us, you'll find it addictive to watch the color materialize from the ball to the project. Have fun.

TIDAL BAY SCARF
By Daniel Zondervan

This is a little crochet project that should let your fingers glide with zing and pure satisfaction. Hook it up, feel it, then wear it. Using Red Heart Unforgettable yarn, the colour changes are stunning. It has stretch and the stitch combination is super easy.

Materials

Red Heart® Unforgettable™ (100g/3.5 oz, 247 m/ 270 yds) - **Sugarcane**, 3 Balls.

Use size 6.5 mm, U.S. K/10.5 crochet hook or size needed to obtain gauge. Measurement approx 8" [20 cm] long x 80" 20" [203 cm] wide. Gauge 14 sc and 16 rows = 4" [10 cm].

Note: To change the size, stitch multiples are 3 + 1.

Instructions

Ch 40.

1st row: (RS) 1 hdc in 3rd chain from hook. Skipped chain doesn't count as st. 1 hdc in each st across. Turn. 38 sts.

2nd row: Ch 2 (doesn't count as stitch), 1 hdc in each st across. Turn. 38 sts.

3rd and 4th rows: Rep 2nd row.

5th set up row: Ch 3 (counts as st here and through-out), *sk next 2 sts, (2 dc, ch 2, 1 sc) in next st. Rep from * across. 1 dc in last st. Turn. 38 sts, ch 2 sps not counted.

6th row: Ch 3, *2 dc in ch 2 sp, ch 2, scfp in 1st dc of the next group of 2. Rep from * across. 1 dc in last st. Turn.

7th to 20th rows: Rep 6th row.

21st row: Ch 2, 1 hdc in same st, *1 hdc in next ch 2 sp, 1 hdc in next 2 dc sts. Rep from * across. 1 hdc in last st. Turn.

22nd to 24th rows: Rep 2nd row.

Rep 5th to 24th rows, 8 more times. Fasten off.

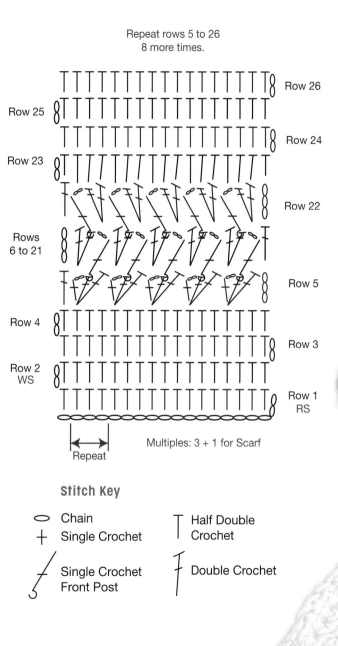

Repeat rows 5 to 26
8 more times.

Row 26
Row 25
Row 24
Row 23
Row 22
Rows 6 to 21
Row 5
Row 4
Row 3
Row 2 WS
Row 1 RS

Repeat

Multiples: 3 + 1 for Scarf

Stitch Key

⬭ Chain

✛ Single Crochet

〤 Single Crochet Front Post

T Half Double Crochet

Ŧ Double Crochet

61

YARN TALES: TIDAL BAY

Nothing is influenced by the landscape around it quite like fine wine. The climate, the natural vegetation that grows in the area, the chemical components of the soil where the grapes grow - all of these factors come together to impart an unique flavour on a particular appellation of wine that's difficult to reproduce. Wine growers call the combination of factors a "terroir."

The great terroirs of the world - Bordeaux, the Châteauneuf Plateau, the Rhone and Napa Valleys - are all famous among wine lovers. And the valley where we live also has a great terroir.

The Annapolis Valley's latitude is similar to that of Bordeaux, France, making it an ideal place to serve as the centre of Nova Scotia's burgeoning wine industry. With 15 to 20 vineyards in operation, as well as cideries popping up regularly, the Valley is Nova Scotia's wine and cider capital.

To promote the fine growing conditions of the province, Nova Scotian wine producers have banded together to develop a distinctive wine appellation called Tidal Bay. Bred from the Annapolis Valley's fertile microclimate and influenced by the highest tides in the world, Tidal Bay is an aromatic white wine that captures the subtle flavours and cool growing conditions of the region. It pairs beautifully with the great seafood that is so abundant in our part of the world.

Winemakers are allowed to choose between 20 identified grape varieties to make Tidal Bay products, but all grapes must be grown and fermented in Nova Scotia. The end product must pass a blind taste test carried out by a panel of experts before it can display the Tidal Bay label.

If you stop by Nova Scotia, give it a try.

TIDAL BAY COWL

Flat or Mobius Designs by Daniel Zondervan with Megan McHugh

Materials

Red Heart® Unforgettable™ (100 g/3.5oz, 247 m/270 yds) - **Rainforest,** 1 Ball

Use size 6.5 mm, U.S. K/10.5 crochet hook or size needed to obtain gauge. Gauge 14 sc and 16 rows = 4" [10 cm]. Measurement approx 7" [18 cm] long x 12" [30.5 cm] dia.

Note: To change the size, stitch multiples are 3.

Cowl in the Round with Optional Mobius Twist

This method is worked back and forth but appears like it is worked in continuous rounds; so once the setup part is done, it is smooth sailing until it is as large as you wish or you run out of yarn.

Choose the start that is most comfortable for you. If you don't want a twist in your cowl, do not do the half twist at the beginning of the project and your cowl will be flat.

Instructions

Beg ch: Loosely, ch 90, careful not to twist the chain. Join with sl st to beg ch to form ring.

Mobius Join

Keep your chain row twist free and join. Continue with the single crochet row. Before joining the last single crochet, give it a half twist so that you are joining at the bottom of the first sc. Continue with pattern.

1st row: (RS) Ch 1, 1 sc in each back hump of ch. When joining, apply a half twist to the chain and join with sl st to beg sc. 90 sts.

When joining Mobius style, the first set up row will begin along the underside after the join. When following it around, you will notice you will pass by the joining again but on the opposite side, so keep on going until you are back to where you had started. You appear to be circling around the Mobius twice in order to get back to the start of a row.

2nd row set up: Ch 3 (counts as st here and throughout), 1 dc, ch 2, 1 sc in same beg st. *sk next 2 sts, (2 dc, ch 2, 1 sc) in next st. Rep from * across until 2 sts left. Join with sl st to top of beg ch 3. Turn. 90 sts.

2nd row: Sl st into next ch 2 sp. Ch 3, 1 dc in same ch 2 sp, ch 2, fpsc in 1st dc

of the next group of 2. *sk next 2 sts, (2 dc in ch 2 sp, ch 2, scfp in 1st dc of the next group of 2). Rep from * across until 2 sts left. Join with sl st to top of beg ch 3. Turn. 90 sts.

Rep 2nd row until cowl measures 7" [18 cm] high.

Fasten off.

Repeat row 3
until recommended length.

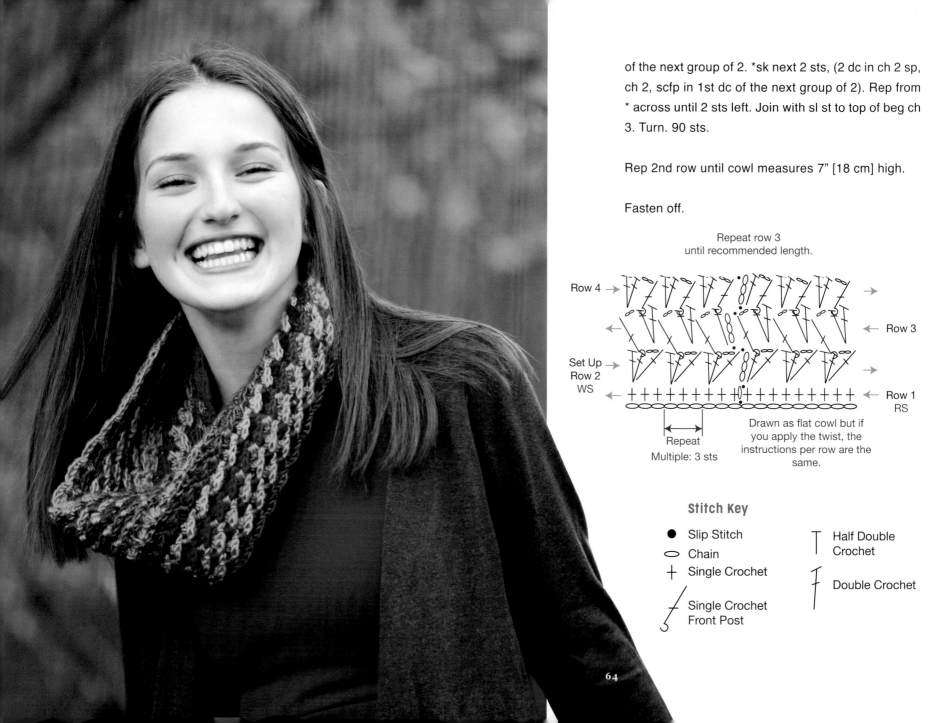

Row 4 →

← Row 3

Set Up
Row 2 →
WS

Row 1 →
RS

Repeat
Multiple: 3 sts

Drawn as flat cowl but if you apply the twist, the instructions per row are the same.

Stitch Key

● Slip Stitch

◯ Chain

✛ Single Crochet

Single Crochet
Front Post

┬ Half Double
Crochet

Double Crochet

64

TIDAL BAY HEADBANDS

Flat or Mobius Designs by Daniel Zondervan with Megan McHugh

Materials

Red Heart® Unforgettable™ (100 g/3.5 oz, 247m/ 270 yds) - Rainforest, 1 Ball. One ball can make 2 headbands.

Use size 6.5 mm, U.S. K/10.5 crochet hook or size needed to obtain gauge. Measurement approx 3" [8 cm] wide x 8" [20 cm] dia.

Note: To change the size, stitch multiples are 3.

Created like the cowl, you need to begin with ch 60. Like the cowl, you can decide if you want the twist or keep the headband flat.

Baby Blanket, With Love

Design by Jeanne Steinhilber

Jeanne wanted easy, repeating stitching patterns for this project so that the baby-sized blanket is reasonably quick to complete. Conscious of tiny toes snagging on stitches, she experimented with the Jacob's Ladder concept of looping the chains to create texture. These loops will pull together, tightening the sides. This also works as a wonderful lapghan for a nursing home or hospital.

Red Heart With Love is soft to the touch and crochets beautifully. The colours are vibrant and the yarn is easy on the hands.

Jeanne is actively involved in charity giving and she is always (and I mean always) one of the first to step up and volunteer. With this particular project, she wanted easy, repeating stitching patterns, so that the baby-sized blanket is reasonably quick to complete. There is always a baby shower or event happening somewhere and this will be a much appreciated gift.

MATERIALS

Red Heart® With Love™ (198 g/7 oz, 338 meters/370 yards)
Contrast A Stone 2 Balls
Contrast B White 1 Ball
Contrast C Wintergreen 1 Ball

Use size 5.5 mm, U.S. I/9 hook or size needed to obtain gauge. Measurements approx 40" x 40" [101 x 101 cm]. Gauge after 5 rounds, the square will be 4.75" [12 cm].

NOTES: This blanket uses hdc join to the beginning stitch at the end of the round, unless otherwise stated.

Stitch counts at the end of an instruction are per side and total stitch count around. Example in *Rnd*

4...5 sc. There are 5 single crochet stitches per side. Each corner with exception to the border has a chain 2 but the first corner is always joined with a hdc which is the equivalent of a chain 2.

Instructions

1st rnd: (RS) With A, ch 2, in 2nd ch from hook, 1 sc, [ch 2, 1 sc] 3 times, join. 4 sc.

2nd rnd: Ch 2 (counts as dc here and throughout), 1 dc in same sp (working around post of hdc), 1 dc in next st, *(2 dc, ch 2, 2 dc) in corner ch 2, 1 dc in next st; rep from * two more times, 2 dc in beg corner, join. 5 dc.

3rd rnd: Ch 1, 1 sc in same sp, *ch 1, sk next st, [1 sc in next st, ch 1, sk next st] to corner ch 2 sp**, (1 sc, ch 2, 1 sc) in corner; rep from * twice, then * to ** once, 1 sc in beg corner, join. Break. 4 sc.

4th rnd: With B, standing sc in any corner ch 2 sp, *ch 1, sk next st, [1 sc in next ch 1 sp, ch 1, sk next st] to corner ch 2 sp**, (1 sc, ch 2, 1 sc) in corner; rep from * twice, then from * to ** once, 1 sc in beg corner, join. 5 sc.

5th rnd: Ch 2, 1 dc in same sp, *1 dc in next st, [sk next ch 1 sp, 1 dc in next st, cross back, 1 dc in skipped sp (X-st made)] to corner ch 2 sp**, (2 dc, ch 2, 2 dc) in corner; rep from * twice, then from * to ** once, 2 dc in beg corner, join. 4 X-st and 5 dc.

6th rnd: Ch 1, 1 sc in same sp, *ch 1, sk next st, [1 sc in next st, ch 1, sk next st] to corner ch 2 sp**, (1 sc, ch 2, 1 sc) in corner; rep from * twice, then * to ** once, 1 sc in beg corner, join. Break. 8 sc.

7th rnd: With C, standing sc in any corner ch 2 sp, *ch 1, sk next st, [1 sc in next ch 1 sp, ch 1, sk next st] to corner ch 2 sp**, (1 sc, ch 2, 1 sc) in corner; rep from * twice, then from * to ** once, 1 sc in beg corner, join. 9 sc.

8th rnd: Ch 2, 1 dc in same sp, *1 dc in each st and ch 1 sp to corner ch 2 sp**, (2 dc, ch 2, 2 dc) in corner; rep from * twice, then from * to ** once, 2 dc in beg corner, join. 21 dc.

9th rnd: Ch 1, 1 sc in same sp, *ch 1, sk next st, [1 sc in next st, ch 1, sk next st] to corner ch 2 sp**, (1 sc, ch 2, 1 sc) in corner; rep from * twice, then * to ** once, 1 sc in beg corner, join. Break. 12 sc.

10th rnd: With A, standing sc in any corner ch 2 sp, *ch 1, sk next st, [1 sc in next ch 1 sp, ch 1, sk next st] to corner ch 2 sp**, (1 sc, ch 2, 1 sc) in corner; rep from * twice, then from * to ** once, 1 sc in beg corner, join. 13 sc.

In round 11, the ch 1 sps from rnd 10 will count as a stitch.

11th rnd: Ch 2, 1 dc in same sp, *ch 8, sk next st, [1 dc in next 5 sts, ch 8, sk next st] to corner ch 2 sp**, (2 dc, ch 2, 2 dc) in corner; rep from * twice, then from * to ** once, 2 dc in beg corner, join. Break. 24 dc and 5 ch-8 loops.

12th rnd: With B, join with sl st in any corner ch 2 sp, ch 2, 1 dc in same sp, *1 dc in next 2 sts, [ch 8, sk ch loop, 1 dc in next 5 sts] until 2 sts to corner ch 2 sp, 1 dc in next 2 sts**, (2 dc, ch 2, 2 dc) in corner; rep from * twice, then from * to ** once, 2 dc in beg corner, join. Break. 28 dc and 5 ch-8 loops.

13th rnd: With C, join with sl st in any corner ch 2 sp, ch 2, 1 dc in same sp, *1 dc in next 4 sts, [ch 8, sk ch loop, 1 dc in next 5 sts] until 4 sts to corner ch 2 sp, 1 dc in next 4 sts**, (2 dc, ch 2, 2 dc) in corner; rep from * twice, then from * to ** once, 2 dc in beg corner, join. Break. 32 dc and 5 ch-8 loops.

14th rnd: With A, join with sl st in any corner ch 2 sp, ch 2, 1 dc in same sp, *1 dc in next 6 sts, sl st into top of twisted loops, [dc in next 5 sts, sl st into top of twisted loops] until 6 sts remain, dc in next 6 sts**, (2 dc, ch 2, 2 dc) in corner; rep from * twice, then from * to ** once, 2 dc in beg corner, join. 36 dc.

15th rnd: Ch 1, sc in same sp, *ch 1, sk next st, [1 sc in next st, ch 1, sk next st] to corner ch 2 sp**, (1 sc, ch 2, 1 sc) in corner; rep from * twice, then * to ** once, 1 sc in beg corner, join. Break. 22 sc.

16th rnd: With B, standing sc in any corner ch 2 sp, *ch 1, sk next st, [1 sc in next ch 1 sp, ch 1, sk next st] to corner ch 2 sp**, (1 sc, ch 2, 1 sc) in corner; rep from * twice, then from * to ** once, 1 sc in beg corner, join. Break. 23 sc.

17th rnd: With C, standing sc in any corner ch 2 sp, *ch 1, sk next st, [1 sc in next ch 1 sp, ch 1, sk next st] to corner ch 2 sp**, (1 sc, ch 2, 1 sc) in corner; rep from * twice, then from * to ** once, 1 sc in beg corner, join. Break. 24 sc.

18th rnd: With A, standing sc in any corner ch 2 sp, *ch 1, sk next st, [1 sc in next ch 1 sp, ch 1, sk next st] to corner ch 2 sp**, (1 sc, ch 2, 1 sc) in corner; rep from * twice, then from * to ** once, 1 sc in beg corner, join. 25 sc.

19th rnd: Ch 2, 1 dc in same sp, *1 dc in each st and ch 1 sp to corner ch 2 sp**, (2 dc, ch 2, 2 dc) in corner; rep from * twice, then from * to ** once, 2 dc in beg corner, join. 53 dc.

20th rnd: Ch 1, sc in same sp, *ch 1, sk next st, [1 sc in next st, ch 1, sk next st] to corner ch 2 sp**, (1 sc, ch 2, 1 sc) in corner; rep from * twice, then * to ** once, 1 sc in beg corner, join. Break. 28 sc.

TIP: The blanket will progressively get bigger and the stitch counts across the sides will increase naturally. If you love this design, you can make it much bigger than a baby size.

Repeat rnds 4 to 20th once. Then rnds 4 to 15 once. Then continue with A and repeat rnd 8.

Final row (51st row): Ch 1, 1 sc in same sp. *1 sc in next st, [Xsc to next corner] rep [ ] to next corner** (1 sc, ch 1, 1 sc) in corner sp; rep from * twice, then from * to ** once more, 1 sc in beg sp, join.

Fasten off.

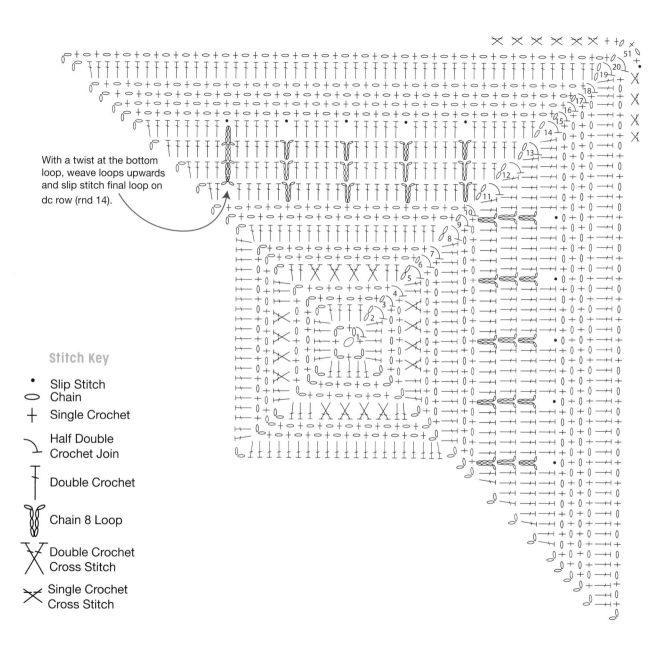

With a twist at the bottom loop, weave loops upwards and slip stitch final loop on dc row (rnd 14).

Stitch Key

- • Slip Stitch
- ○ Chain
- + Single Crochet
- ⌐ Half Double Crochet Join
- ⊤ Double Crochet
- ⌇ Chain 8 Loop
- ✕ Double Crochet Cross Stitch
- ⤬ Single Crochet Cross Stitch

YARN TALES: YARN, THE SOURCE OF OUR ART

Yarn aisles are endless possibilities of creativity waiting to be unleashed.

At first I would look at the ball and judge it by the price tag, not factoring in the cost of production, the type of fibres and the artistic value. But over the years I've learned to appreciate a wide range of fibres and the processes that went into their manufacturing.

As well as old-fashioned favourites, the industry has introduced new and unusual products like Qiviuk made from the delicate underwool of the Arctic muskox.

You're the artists. Use what you love and love what you do.

Furrows in the Valley Hat

Design by Yarnspirations

You can never have enough hats and the variety of yarn, textures and colours on the market create a candy land for fashion. This ribbed hat is available in three sizes, from toddler to adult. Using Bernat Softee Chunky Tweeds makes it quick to complete, perfect for gift and charity box donations. Because of the super easy repeating this project can be completed in an evening.

Materials

Bernat® Softee Chunky Tweeds™ (300 g/10.5 oz, 298 m/316 yds) one ball - **Blue Tweed,** one ball.

Use size 8 mm, U.S. L/11 crochet hook or size needed to obtain gauge. Measurements: Child 2/4 years 19" [48 cm] circumference; Child 6/10 years 20" [51 cm] circum-ference; Adult 21-22" [53.5-56 cm]. Gauge 8 sc and 9 rows = 4" [10 cm].

NOTES

- The instructions are written for the smallest size. If changes are necessary for larger size(s) the instructions will be written thus ( ). Numbers for each size are shown in the same color throughout the pattern. When only one number is given in black, it applies to all sizes.

- Hat is worked side to side. Ch 2 at beg of row does not count as st.

Instructions

Ch 23 (28-32) leaving a 24" [61 cm] long end for seaming later.

1st row: (RS) 1 hdc in 3rd ch from hook. 1 hdc in each of next 15 (19-22) ch. 1 sc in each of last 5 (6-7) ch. Turn. 21 (26-30) sts.

2nd row: Ch 1. Working in front loops only, 1 sc in each of rst 5 (6-7) sc. *Work 1 hdc into horizontal bar created below st in the previous row (bar is below loops normally worked – see diagram). Rep from * to end of row. Turn.

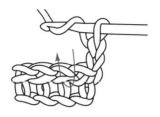

3rd row: Ch 2. *Work 1 hdc into horizontal bar created below st in the previous row (bar is below loops normally worked). Rep from * 15 (19-22) times more. Working in front loops only, 1 sc in each of last 5 (6-7) sc. Turn.

Rep last 2 rows until hat (at widest point) measures approx 17 (18- 19)" [43 (45.5-48) cm] ending on a 2nd row. Fasten off.

Final Touches and Pom Pom

Using end from foundation ch, weave yarn through short side of hat (sc rows) and gather the top of hat tog securely. Sew center back seam. Turn back cuff as shown.

Pompom: Wind yarn around 3 (4-4) fingers approx 70 (80-80) times. Remove from fingers and tie tightly in centre. Cut through each side of loops. Trim to a smooth round shape, approx 3 (4-4)" [7.5 (10-10) cm] diameter. Sew to top of hat.

YARN TALES: CROCHET KEEPS US WELL

One thing is certain about crochet. It makes you feel better. Most crocheters already know this, but now a study by the University of Wollongong in Australia has confirmed it.

The study found that "crochet offers positive benefits for personal well-being with many people actively using crochet to manage mental health conditions and life events such as grief, chronic illness and pain." Titled Happy Hookers, the study surveyed almost 8,400 crocheters in 87 countries.

The three biggest reasons for crocheting among people who took part in the survey were: to be creative (82 per cent), to relax (78 per cent) and for a sense of accomplishment (75 per cent.) Almost 90 per cent said crochet made them feel calmer, 82 per cent saying it made them happier, and 75 per cent saying it made them feel more useful.

Crocheters also said that crocheting regularly improved their memory and concentration and helped them forget pain or other problems. Some 60 to 74 per cent said the craft also boosted their confidence and self-esteem. And some even said they use crochet to deal with diagnoses such as anxiety, depression and eating disorders.

The survey also found that people who participated in online crochet communities (Hey, that's us!) had stronger relationships and made more friends through crochet. It's always nice when your obsession happens to be good for your health.

Don't stress out about your crochet skill level. I am always learning new things. Where's the fun in knowing everything right off the bat? I've been crocheting for more than three decades (pass the Oil of Olay!) and I still learn something every day.

I'm just really passionate about what I do. Embrace the skills you have instead of what you think you're missing. Your creativity is unique to you. It's not about speed, it's about your own desire to learn, practice and grow. It's a hobby, not a race. Someone will always be a stronger crocheter than you, just like you'll always be stronger than somebody else. And that's a great thing, because it shows you can keep growing, and help others with their skills.

Nor'easter Hat

Design by Yarnspirations

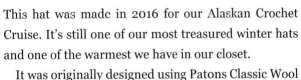

This hat was made in 2016 for our Alaskan Crochet Cruise. It's still one of our most treasured winter hats and one of the warmest we have in our closet.

It was originally designed using Patons Classic Wool Roving. Look for a chunky weight #5 yarn and crochet your own colour scheme. Pick up the pom-pom at the craft store or make your own.

Each colour requires just one ball in the brands recommended.

Materials

Patons® ClassicWoolRoving™(100g/3.5oz,109m/1 20 yds). **Bernat® Softee Chunky**™ (100 g/3.5 oz, 99 m/108 yds)
Contrast A - Main Colour, 1 Ball
Contrast B - Secondary Colour, 1 Ball

Use sizes 6.5 mm, U.S. K/10 hook and 8 mm, U.S. L/11 hook or size needed to obtain gauge. Measurements: Average adult size hat. Gauge: 8 dc and 4 rows = 4" [10 cm] with larger hook and Patons Classic Wool Roving.

NOTES

- Do not break colors. Carry color not in use loosely up WS of work. To change colors, work to last 2 loops on hook of first color. Yoh with new color and draw through rem 2 loops and proceed.

Instructions

Ribbing - Brim

With smaller hook and B, ch 10.

1st row: (RS) Turn chain sideways and working into back loops of chain, sl st in 2nd ch from hook. Sl st in each ch to end of chain. Turn. 9 sts.

2nd row: Ch 1. Working into back loops only, sl st in each sl st to end of row. Join A. Turn.

3rd and 4th rows: With A, as 2nd row. Join B.

5th and 6th rows: With B, as 2nd row. Join A.

Rep 3rd to 6th rows until ribbing (when slightly stretched) measures approx 18½" [47 cm], ending on a 4th row. Do not fasten off.

Join ends: Place RS tog and working through both thicknesses, with B, work 1 row of sl st through back loops of final row and rem loops of foundation ch. Fasten off.

Hat

With RS facing and smaller hook, join A with sl st at center back seam of Ribbing. Ch 1. Work 41 sc evenly around top edge (where colours were carried) of Ribbing. Join B with sl st to first sc. Place marker on last sc. Change to larger hook.

1st rnd: With B, ch 3 (counts as dc). Work 1 dc in each st around. Join A with sl st to top of ch 3.

2nd rnd: With A, ch 2 (counts as st). *Cr Dcfp. Rep from * around. Join B with sl st to top of ch 2. Rep last 2 rnds for pat until work from marker measures 4" [10 cm], ending with a 2nd rnd.

Shape top

1st rnd: With B, ch 3 (counts as dc). *Dc2tog. 1 dc in each of next 2 sts. Rep from * around. Join A with sl st to top of ch 3. 31 sts.

2nd rnd: With A, ch 2 (counts as st). *Cr Dcfp. Rep from * around. Join B with sl st to top of ch 2.

3rd rnd: With B, ch 3 (counts as dc). *Dc2tog. 1 dc in next st. Rep from * around. Join A with sl st to top of ch 3. 21 sts.

4th rnd: As 2nd rnd.

5th rnd: With B, ch 3 (counts as dc). *Dc2tog. Rep from * around. Join with sl st to top of ch 3. 11 sts. Fasten off leaving a long end. Thread end onto tapestry needle and weave end tightly through rem sts.
Fasten securely.

Optional Handmade Pompom

Wind A around 4 fingers approx 100 times. Tie tightly in the middle, leaving a long end for attaching to hat. Cut loops at both ends, and trim to a smooth round shape. Sew to top of hat. Or purchase a ready-made pom-pom

Tidal Wedge Wrap

Design by Anita Grover

Anita has two colour-combination versions of her Tunisian Tidal Wedge Wrap. Both are exactly the same wrap, but they look completely different. One is solid and subtle and the other is fun and unconventional. The key to this project is to find a thin yarn. A super fine #1 is best.

If you are new to Tunisian, we have tutorials for starting this amazing skill set. It's a mixture of crochet and knitting, adopting techniques from both realms.

Materials

Patons® Kroy Socks™ (50 g/1.75 oz, 152 m/166 yds) - **Contrast A** Flax, 6 Balls
Patons® Kroy Socks FX™ (50 g/1.75 oz, 152 m/166 yds) - **Contrast B** Cascade Colors, 6 Balls

Alternative Option - Checkerboard Version
Patons® Kroy Socks FX™ (50 g/1.75 oz, 152 m/166 yds) - **Contrast A** Cadet Colors, 6 Balls
Patons® Kroy Socks™ (50 g/1.75 oz, 152 m/166 yds) - **Contrast B** Muslin, 6 Balls

Use Afghan Hook approx. 11" long or cable if you prefer. Size 8 mm, U.S. L/11 hook. Measurements: 72 long" x 21 wide" [183 x 53 cm]. Gauge 12 sts and 11 rows = 4" [10 cm] in Tunisian Simple Stitch. Use any size hook to obtain the gauge.

TIPS:
- Do not turn work. Always work on front side.
- End of row (last stitch); go through both vertical strands of stitch.
- Use same colour for one forward and return pass.
- On the last wedge do not do Row 38. Simply Bind off down the side of the wedge to the end.
- Use Tunisian abbreviation stitch definitions. (See back of book.)

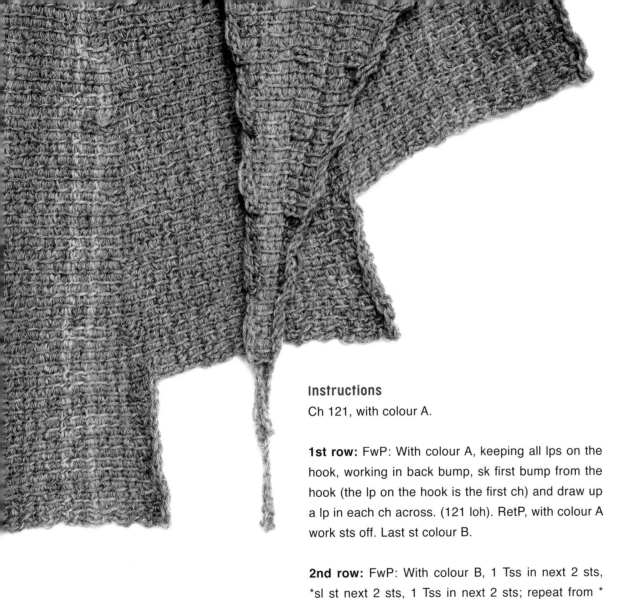

3rd row: FwP: With colour B, 1 Tss in next 2 sts, *sl st next 2 sts, 1 Tss in next 2 sts; repeat from * across. (115 loh). RetP, with colour B work sts off. Last st colour A.

4th row: FwP: With colour A, *sl st next 2 sts, 1 Tss in next 2 sts; repeat from * across leaving 6 sts unworked. (109 loh). RetP, with colour A work sts off. Last st colour A.

5th row: FwP: With colour A, *sl st next 2 sts, 1 Tss in next 2 sts; repeat from * across. (109 loh). RetP, with colour A work sts off. Last st colour B.

6th row: FwP: With colour B, 1 Tss in next 2 sts, *sl st next 2 sts, 1 Tss in next 2 sts; repeat from * across leaving last 6 sts unworked. (103 loh). RetP, with colour B work sts off.

7th row: FwP: With colour B, 1 Tss in next 2 sts, *sl st next 2 sts, 1 Tss in next 2 sts; repeat from * across. (103 loh). RetP, with colour B work sts off. Last st colour A.

8th row: Rep row 4; colour A. (97 loh)
9th row: Rep row 5; colour A. (97 loh)
10th row: Rep row 6; colour B. (91 loh)
11th row: Rep row 7; colour B. (91 loh)

Instructions
Ch 121, with colour A.

1st row: FwP: With colour A, keeping all lps on the hook, working in back bump, sk first bump from the hook (the lp on the hook is the first ch) and draw up a lp in each ch across. (121 loh). RetP, with colour A work sts off. Last st colour B.

2nd row: FwP: With colour B, 1 Tss in next 2 sts, *sl st next 2 sts, 1 Tss in next 2 sts; repeat from * across leaving last 6 sts unworked. (115 loh). RetP, with colour B work sts off.

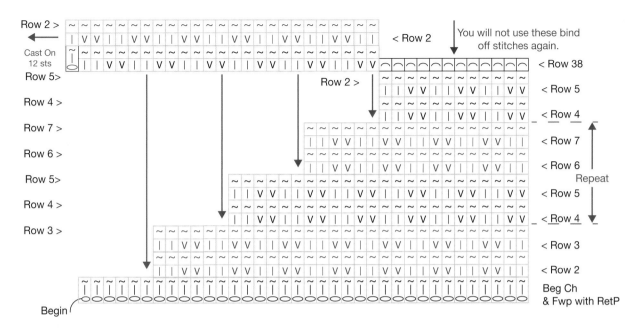

Stitch Key

~ /	Beg Ch with Fwp with RetP
⬭	
		Tunisian Simple Stitch
~	Return Pass
V	Slip Stitch
⌒	Bind Off
↓	Where to Collect Stitches

(Chart labels: Row 2 >, Cast On 12 sts, Row 5>, Row 4 >, Row 7 >, Row 6 >, Row 5>, Row 4 >, Row 3 >, Begin, < Row 2, You will not use these bind off stitches again, < Row 38, < Row 5, < Row 4, < Row 7, < Row 6, Repeat, < Row 5, < Row 4, < Row 3, < Row 2, Beg Ch & Fwp with RetP, Row 2 >)

12th row: Rep row 4; colour A. (85 loh)

13th row: Rep row 5; colour A. (85 loh)

14th row: Rep row 6; colour B. (79 loh)

15th row: Rep row 7; colour B. (79 loh)

16th row: Rep row 4; colour A. (73 loh)

17th row: Rep row 5; colour A. (73 loh)

18th row: Rep row 6; colour B. (67 loh)

19th row: Rep row 7; colour B. (67 loh)

20th row: Rep row 4; colour A. (61 loh)

21st row: Rep row 5; colour A. (61 loh)

22nd row: Rep row 6; colour B. (55 loh)

23rd row: Rep row 7; colour B. (55 loh)

24th row: Rep row 4; colour A. (49 loh)

25th row: Rep row 5; colour A. (49 loh)

26th row: Rep row 6; colour B. (43 loh)

27th row: Rep row 7; colour B. (43 loh)

28th row: Rep row 4; colour A. (37 loh)

29th row: Rep row 5; colour A. (37 loh)

30th row: Rep row 6; colour B. (31 loh)

31st row: Rep row 7; colour B. (31 loh)

32nd row: Rep row 4; colour A. (25 loh)

33rd row: Rep Row 5; colour A. (25 loh)

34th row: Rep row 6; colour B. (19 loh)

35th row: Rep row 7; colour B. (19 loh)

36th row: Rep row 4; colour A. (13 loh)

37th row: Rep row 5; colour A. (13 loh)

11 Wedges

Next Wedge Builds onto Last Wedge

Begin Here with Wedge

Wedge Building

TIP: When something doesn't exist, invent a name. The cast on at the end of row 38 requires you to add 12 more loops to the hook, but the only yarn you can play with is leading to the yarn ball. Anita came up with the name of Yarn Ball Cast On.

Yarn Ball Cast On: Similar to the way Long Tail Cast On is for knitting, the long tail in this case is leading to the yarn ball itself. Use the same principles of knitting to cast on these additional loops needed to proceed.

38th row: With colour A, *slip stitch bind off next 12 sts, *slip 2 sts and 2 Tss*; repeat down the wedge to first row. Cast 12 sts on hook. (121 loh). RetP, with colour A work sts off. Last st colour B.

Rep rows 2 to 38 until you have a total of 11 wedges. Don't be afraid to add more wedges if you prefer.

* On the final wedge **DO NOT DO 38th row.** Simply Bind off down the side of the wedge to the end. Fasten off and weave in ends.

Wet or damp block your new wrap for best presentation when wearing.

YARN TALES: CROCHET BY THE NUMBERS

◇ Thirty million Americans participate in knitting and/or crochet. Did you know that Latin America is booming in crochet yarn arts? There are more Spanish speaking *YouTube* hosts popping up. With the help of our Closed Captioning Team and also several volunteers, with the click of a button on *YouTube*, our videos can be translated instantly to over 35 global languages and available to the deaf and hard of hearing global communities. Isn't that a great way to get people to participate in crochet?

◇ Crochet and knitting accounts for almost $3 billion in the U.S. craft market, with an average monthly spend per household of $20.57. If I were to only spend that much, I would have to be on a serious yarn diet! NOT HAPPENING! Canadians also spend more per household on yarn than Americans at the cash register.

◇ Seventy-seven per cent buy their supplies in a physical store. Four per cent buy outside physical stores, and 19 per cent buy from both. With the rise of the pandemic and online shopping, we predict these numbers will drastically change. But nothing replaces a good feel in the yarn aisle.

◇ Sixty-two per cent give their projects as gifts. Crochet and knit items are the most commonly donated crafts. Like the Energizer Bunny, it keeps giving and giving and giving. The COVID-19 pandemic of 2020 created a two-fold scenario; giving items to charities has been more difficult but an increase of crocheted gifts for family and friends has increased.

◇ Eighteen per cent of crocheters and knitters consider themselves experts, while the other 82 per cent rate their skills as beginner to intermediate. Learning a new skill never ends for anyone. Never underestimate your skills. Don't devalue yourself; you know more than what you believe.

◇ The current statistical data shows 71 per cent of knitters and crocheters are female and 29 per cent are male. Times are changing and the communities of LGBTQIA2S+ (Lesbian, Gay, Bisexual, Transgender, Questioning, Intersex, Asexual and Two-Spirit) are requesting more equality. We suspect a more inclusive breakdown in statistical data will occur in the future but for now, we are unsure of those numbers.

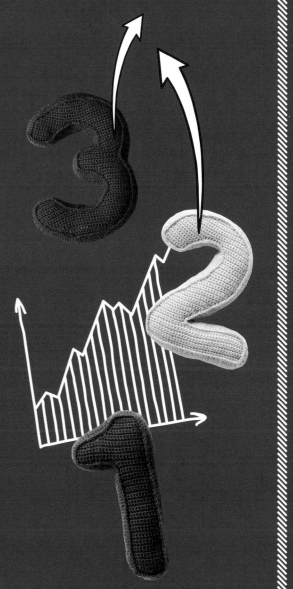

Heritage Nova Scarf

Design by Daniel Zondervan

If there is one thing Canadians know, it's winter. The color combination of the Heritage Scarf can be seen in many fashionable items way up here but it can be just as stunning in the colours of your country. Using Bernat Chunky weight yarn, this project is super fast. The texture is SUPER awesome.

There are some unusual stitches. The D-link crochet stitch is a lot like doing Entrelac or Tunisian. It's one of Diva Dan's favourites.

Materials

Bernat® Softee Chunky™ (300 g/10.5 oz, 298 m /316 yds) - **Contrast A** True Gray Tweed, 2 Balls
Bernat® Softee Chunky™ (100g/5 oz, 99 m /108 yds) - **Contrast B** Wine, 1 Ball
Bernat® Softee Chunky™ (400 g/14 oz, 394 m /431 yds) - **Contrast C** Natural, 1 Ball

Use size 10 mm, U.S. N crochet hook. Measurements approx 13" x 40" [101 x 101 cm]. Gauge is not important.

Special Stitches

D-Link is done in 2 steps.

Step 1 (preparing the tower): Ch 7, Insert hook into 2nd ch from the hook, yoh, and draw through. Cont gathering sts from all remaining chs in this manner. Insert hook into beginning st, yoh and pull through, 8 sts on hook. Finish tower by working as normal dc; yoh, draw through two and cont to draw through to final 2 sts.

Step 2: Insert hook into top horizontal bar of previous st, yoh, pull through. Cont with remaining horizontal bars to bottom 7 loops on hook before going into the next st. Once gone through next st on main body of pattern you have 8 loops on hook and go through 2 loops 7x. Insert hook into next st, yoh, pull through. Finish tower by working as normal dc; yoh, draw through two and cont to draw through to final two sts. Repeat Step 2 to last stitch

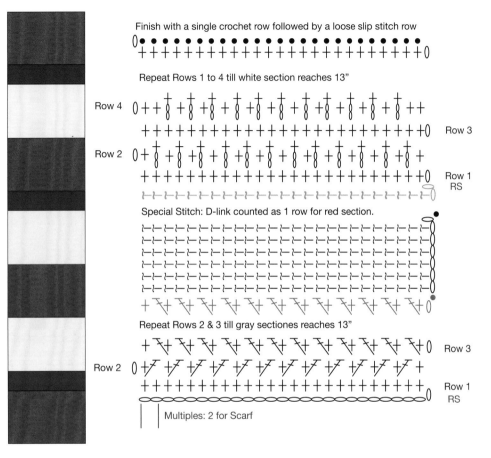

Finish with a single crochet row followed by a loose slip stitch row

Repeat Rows 1 to 4 till white section reaches 13"

Row 4

Row 3

Row 2

Row 1
RS

Special Stitch: D-link counted as 1 row for red section.

Repeat Rows 2 & 3 till gray sectiones reaches 13"

Row 3

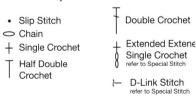

Row 2

Row 1
RS

Multiples: 2 for Scarf

Stitch Key

- • Slip Stitch
- ⌒ Chain
- + Single Crochet
- ⊤ Half Double Crochet
- ⊤ Double Crochet
- ⊤ Extended Extene Single Crochet
  refer to Special Stitch
- ⊢ D-Link Stitch
  refer to Special Stitch

Bobblet Stitch

Insert hook in next stitch. Yarn over, pull through loop. Yarn over, pull through one loop only. Yarn over again, pull through one loop. Final yarn over and pull through two loops. Bobblet Stitch is made. Take note when working with the Bobblet Stitch you will want to start on the RS of the project so that the texture can be seen. So the first row of bobblet sts will be worked on the WS. (They do pop out onto the RS which is the look you want to achieve.)

Notes

- This scarf is worked by sections. The stitch count will always be 25 sts across.
- Follow colour diagram.

Instructions

Gray Section

With A, ch 26.

1st row: (RS) 1 sc in 2nd ch from hook. 1 sc in each st across.

2nd row: Ch 1, (1 sc, 1 dc in the same st), *sk next st, (1 sc, 1 dc in next st). Rep from * to last 2 sts. Sk next st, 1 sc in final st. Turn. 25 sts.

Rep 2nd row until approx 13" [33 cm] ending on the end of RS. Break.

Red Section

1st row: (RS) With B, follow Special Instructions for D-link. Break. 25 sts.

White Section

1st row: (RS) With C, attach to beg st, ch 1. 1 sc into each st across. Turn. 25 sts.

2nd row: Ch 1, *1 sc in first st, 1 ext ext sc in next st. *1 sc in next st, 1 ex ex sc in next st. Rep from * across. 1 sc in last st. Turn. 25 sts.

3rd row: Ch 1, 1 sc into st across. Turn. 25 sts.

4nd row: Ch 1, 1 sc in first st, *1 sc in next st, 1 ex ex sc in next st. Rep from * across to 2 last sts. 1 sc in last 2 sts. Turn. 25 sts.

Rep 1st to 4th rows in rows in white section until approx 13" [33 cm]. Break.

Rep Instructions Throughout Remaining Project

Rep 2nd row of gray section for another 13" [33 cm]
Rep White Section
Rep Red Section
Rep 2nd row of gray section for another 13" [33 cm]
Rep White Section
Rep Red Section
Rep 2nd row of gray section for another 13" [33 cm], ending on WS. Do not fasten off.

Finish

1st row: (RS) Ch 1, 1 sc in each st across. Turn. 25 sts.

2nd row: Ch 1, loosely 1 sl st in each st across. Fasten off.

You will have enough yarn to add an optional fringe.

Cold Cove Hat

Design by Kathleen Neborak Nolen

In the middle of winter when the days are short and the trees are bare, a splash of colour goes a long way to brighten your mood. The technicolours in this hat naturally come out of the ball and give the hat an artisan look and feel. Top it with a ready-made or handmade pom-pom.

The hat has a beautiful texture, and using back posts, it pulls together those double crochets.

Materials

Red Heart® Hello Gorgeous™ (141 g/5 oz, 215 m/236 yds) - **Cactus Flower**, 1 Ball

Use size 5.5 mm, U.S. I/9 and 5 mm, H/8 hook or size needed size to obtain gauge with larger hook. Measurement approx 11" [28 cm] dia. x 9" [23 cm] tall without pom-pom. Gauge 13 dc sts x 8 rows = 4" [10 cm].

NOTE:

- We have videos on magic rings/adjustable rings on *YouTube* if you need extra help to get started.

Instructions

Begin with larger hook.

1st rnd: (RS) 12 dc in magic ring, join with sl st. 12 sts.

2nd rnd: Ch 2, (does not count as st, here and through-out) 2 dc in each st, join with sl st to first dc st. 24 sts.

3rd rnd: Ch 2, *1 dc in first dc, 2 dc in next dc. Rep from * around. Join with sl st to first dc. 36 sts.

4th rnd: Ch 2, *1 dc in next 2 sts, 2 dc in next sts. Rep from * around. Join with sl st to beg dc. 48 sts.

5th rnd: Ch 2, *1 dc in next 3 sts, 2 dc in next st. Rep from * around. Join with sl st to beg dc. 60 sts.

6th rnd: Ch 1, 1 sc in each st around. Join with sl st to beg sc. 60 sts.

7th rnd: Ch 1, 1 scbp in each st around. Join with sl st to beg sc. 60 sts.

8th rnd: Ch 2, *1 dc in next 4 sts, 2 dc in next st. Rep from * around. Join with sl st to beg dc. 72 sts.

9th rnd: Ch 1, 1 sc in each st around. Join with sl st to beg sc. 72 sts.

10th rnd: Ch 1, 1 scbp in each st around. Join with sl st to beg sc. 72 sts.

11th rnd: Ch 2, 1 dc in next 5 sts, 2 dc in next st. Rep from * around. Join with sl st to beg dc. 84 sts.

12th rnd: Ch 1, 1 sc in each st around. Join with sl st to beg sc. 84 sts.

13th rnd: Ch 1, 1 scbp in each st around. Join with sl st to beg sc. 84 sts.

14th rnd: Ch 2, 1 dc in each st around. Join with sl st to beg dc. 84 sts.

15th to 17th rnds: Rep rnds 12 to 14. 84 sts.

18th and 19th rnds: Rep rnds 12 and 13. Do not fasten off.

Brim
Change to smaller hook.

20th to 22nd rnds: Ch 1, *1 dcfp around next st, 1 dcbp around next st. Rep from * around. Join with sl st to beg dcfp. 84 sts.

23rd rnd: Ch 1. 1 sc in each st around. Join with sl st to beg sc. Fasten off. One suggestion is to bow tie a pom-pom to the top of the hat. If you tie it, it can be removed easily if the hat needs to be washed.

Cozy Maritime Wrap

Design by Anita Grover

Anita Grover was determined to figure out how to do a wave in Tunisian crochet and make it look wonderful. She did and this Cozy Maritime Wrap with Red Heart Roll With It Melange is simply stunning.

A misstep with a crochet stitch can be an opportunity to create a new stitch. Anita thought hard, frogged a lot, and by gosh, she achieved a wave that looks amazing and the stitch texture literally popped off the wrap.

Now you can enjoy this stunning wrap too.

Materials

Red Heart® Roll With It Melange™ (150 g /5.29 oz, 356 m/389 yds) - **Theater**, 3 Balls

Use afghan hook approx 11" long or cable hook if you prefer. Size 8 mm, U.S. L/11 hook. Measurements are 100" long x 19" wide [254 x 48 cm]. Gauge is 12 sts and 10 rows = 4" [10 cm] in Tunisian Simple Stitch. Use any size hook to obtain the gauge.

TIPS:

- To change size of shawl: Multiples of 17+2.
- Do not turn work. Always work on front side.
- End of row (last st); go through both vertical strands of stitch.
- Use the Tunisian stitch abbreviations list. (See back of book.)

Stitch Key

○	Chain	│	Tunisian Simple Stitch
φ	Full Stitch	0	Yarn Over
~	Return Pass	⟍	Tss 2 Tog

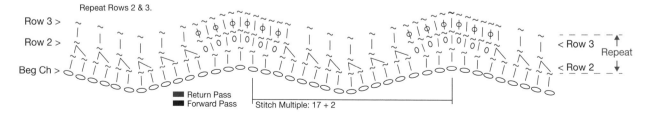

90

Instructions

Ch 70.

1st row: FwP: Keeping all lps on the hook, working in back bump skip first bump from the hook (the lp on the hook is the first ch) and draw up a lp in each ch across. (70 loh). **RetP.**

2nd row: FwP: *(Tss2tog) three times, (yo,tss) five times, yo, (tss2tog) three times*. Last st; go through both vertical strands of stitch. (70 loh). **RetP.**

3rd row: FwP:* (Tss) three times, (tfs,tss) five times, tfs, (tss) three times*. Last st; go through both vertical strands of stitch. (70 loh). **RetP.**

Repeat 2nd and 3rd row until approx 100" [254 cm] in length.

Last Row: Bind off.

Ripples in the Bay Throw

Design by Jeanne Steinhilber

The right colours give Jeanne Steinhilber's throw a marvellous, rippling texture. At first glance, it seems as though the throw has a crochet chain weaved throughout the shells. Jeanne cleverly used a single crochet back post, rippling out more texture and giving the throw a weaved look. Standing back from the throw, you can imagine a pebble dropping in a pond of still water.

This is a project with an easy, repeating stitch. And, like any crochet project, you can stitch and customize it in any way you wish.

Materials

Red Heart® With Love™ (198 g/7 oz, 338 m/370 yds)

Version 1

Aran, 6 Balls

Version 2

White 4 Balls, **Cerulean** 2 Balls

Use size 6 mm, U.S. J/10 hook or size needed to obtain gauge. Measurements approx 53" x 53" [135 x 135 cm]. Gauge should have approx 5" [12.5 cm] after completing round 3.

NOTES

Shell = 3 dc, ch 1, 3 dc in same st.

This pattern uses hdc join to the first stitch of the round when finishing a round.

Stitch counts at the end of instructions are per side. Example in Rnd 2... 7 dc. That is 7 double crochet per side. In *Rnd 3...1 shell, 4 dc*. There is one shell stitch and 4 double crochet.

Instructions - Version 1 (solid colour)

1st rnd: (RS) Ch 4, in 1st ch, 2 dc, [ch 2, 3 dc] 3 times, join. 3 dc per side, 4 ch 2 corners.

2nd rnd: Ch 3 (counts as dc here and throughout), 1 dc in same sp (working around post of hdc), *1 dc in each st to corner,** (2 dc, ch 2s, 2 dc) in corner ch 2; rep from * twice, then * to ** once, 2 dc in beg corner, join. 7 dc.

3rd rnd: Ch 3, 1 dc in same sp, *sk 3 sts, 1 shell in next st, sk 3 sts**, (2 dc, ch 2, 2 dc) in ch 2 sp; rep from * twice, then * to ** once, 2 dc in beg corner, join. 1 shell, 4 dc.

4th rnd: Ch 1, 1 sc in same sp, *1 sc in next 2 sts, 1 scbp in next 3 sts, 1 sc in ch 1 sp, 1 scbp in next 3 sts, 1 sc in next 2 sts,** (1 sc, ch 2, 1 sc) in ch 2 sp; rep from * twice, then * to ** once, 1 sc in beg corner, join. 13 sts.

5th rnd: Ch 3. 1 dc in same sp, *1 dc in each st to corner,** (2 dc, ch 2, 2 dc) in ch 2 sp; rep from * twice, then * to ** once, 2 dc in beg corner, join. 17 dc.

6th rnd: Ch 3, 1 dc in same sp, *sk 3 sts, 1 shell in next st, sk 3 sts, 1 dc in next 3 sts, sk 3 sts, 1 shell in next st, sk 3 sts,** (2 dc, ch 2, 2 dc) in ch 2 sp; rep from * twice, then * to ** once, 2 dc in beg corner, join. 2 shells, 7 dc.

7th rnd: Ch 1, 1 sc in same sp, *1 sc in next 2 sts, 1 scbp in next 3 sts, 1 sc in ch 1 sp, 1 scbp in next 3 sts, 1 sc in next 3 sts, 1 scbp in next 3 sts, 1 sc in ch 1 sp, 1 scbp in next 3 sts, 1 sc in next 2 sts,** (1 sc, ch 2, 1 sc) in ch 2 sp; rep from * twice, then * to ** once, 1 sc in beg corner, join. 23 sc.

YARN TALES: BIGGER THAN KNITTING ... OR BREAD

Crochet has been popular for a long time but it finally overtook knitting in Google search rankings in 2011. By 2014 it was one of the top search trends on *Google*, and almost 30 million Americans were either knitting or crocheting by 2016. But it was during the 2020 global pandemic that the popularity of crochet really surged. With everybody locked down at home, there's only so much bread you can bake, and eat. Ugh. Don't we know it?

The pandemic lockdown caused crochet and other fibre crafts to boom, especially in Spain, France and South America, where crochet trended higher than bread on *Google*. We could actually track it on our *YouTube* channel. When the lockdowns happened, we saw the spike in our traffic literally the next day.

But just like flour and yeast, yarn was hard to get. It turns out there are lots of yarn hoarders among us. Yarn demand was way up in spring 2020, but supply was down because the top four producers of wool for craft yarn - Australia, China, the U.S. and New Zealand - were all hit by the pandemic, combined with international trading and oil pricing. There is far more than meets the eye in the production of a yarn ball. We see yarn on the shelves but don't really comprehend its journey to get there.

Still, supply problems didn't seem to affect the crafters' appetites. Mega crafting companies reported a 15 per cent increase in demand with new people wanting to learn for the very first time.

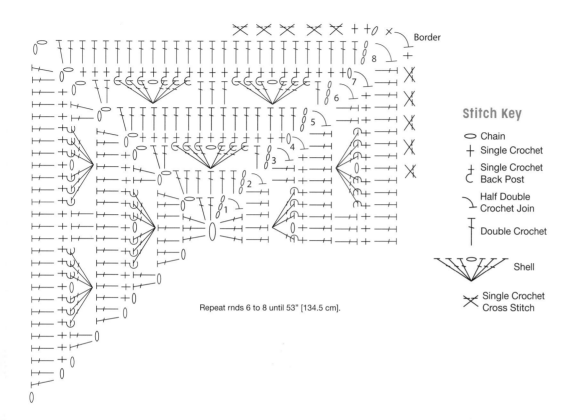

Stitch Key

⬯ Chain

╂ Single Crochet

╆ Single Crochet
C Back Post

⌐ Half Double
  Crochet Join

╁ Double Crochet

⟋⟍ Shell

✕ Single Crochet
  Cross Stitch

Repeat rnds 6 to 8 until 53" [134.5 cm].

8th rnd: Ch 3. 1 dc in same sp, *1 dc in each st to corner,** (2 dc, ch 2, 2 dc) in ch 2 sp; rep from * twice, then * to ** once, 2 dc in beg corner, join. 27 dc.

Rep 6th to 8th rnds until throw measures 53" [134.5 cm] square.

Border: Ch 1, 1 sc in same sp, *1 sc in next st, Xst to corner,** (1 sc, ch 2, 1 sc) in ch 2 sp; rep from * twice,

then * to ** once, 1 sc in beg corner, join. Fasten off. Damp block finished afghan to shape and enjoy.

Version 2 is completed by changing to contrasting color for every single crochet round. It is smaller, measuring 48" x 48" [122 x 122 cm].

Into the Light Afghan

Design by Jeanne Steinhilber

The textures of light bouncing from this one-of-a-kind crochet afghan are amazing. The project was a coping mechanism for Jeanne as she designed this to reach for the light. It is at those times that Jeanne is at her design best. This afghan isn't just a special pattern for this book, it's a piece of her journey.

Materials

Caron Cakes (249 g/8.5 oz, 407 m/445 yds) - **Dusted Cream**, 7 balls

Use 5.5 mm, U.S. I/9 hook or size to obtain gauge. Measurements Approx 60" x 60" [152 x 152 cm]. Gauge is 12 sc and 14 rows = 4" [10 cm].

Special Stitch

The popcorn stitch used here can be different stitch counts depending on project and designer.

Popcorn (pc) = Work 4 dc into the next st, drop loop from the hook, insert your hook from front to back under the top 2 loops of the first double crochet of the group, grab the dropped loop and pull through; 1 pc made.

NOTES:

- Afghan is always worked on RS.
- All stitch counts per side.
- This pattern uses hdc joins when finishing rounds unless otherwise stated.
- Jeanne has provided instructions where there are repeats. Stitch counts per round are provided. Instructions such as, **25th and 26th rnds:** *As 7th and 8th rnds. 81 sc is the 25th rnd and 83 sc is the 26th rnd.* The stitch counts are in order of the round numbers. 81 sc per side is for rnd 7 and 83 sc per side is rnd 8.

Instructions

Ch 4, sl st in beg ch to form ring.

Centre Bavarian Section

1st rnd: Ch 1, *1 sc in ring, ch 5, tr4tog in ring, ch 5; rep from * 3 more times, join. 4 quarter bottom wheels.

2nd rnd: Ch 1, 1 sc in same st as join, *[ch 1, 4 tr top of the tr4tog] 3 times, ch 1**, 1 sc in next sc; rep from * twice, then from * to ** once, join. Break yarn. 4 corner wheels.

YARN TALES: HOW CROCHET HELPED SAVE IRELAND: A BRIEF HISTORY

In 1846, 18-year-old Eleonore Riego de la Branchardiëre published her first book, "Knitting, Crochet and Netting." It quickly became a bestseller and made her the first crochet superstar in the process. Born in France, Branchardiëre was Irish on her mother's side, and she incorporated the fine crochet lace of Ireland into her popular designs. She had a knack for turning needle and bobbin lace designs into crochet patterns that could be easily duplicated.

Branchardiëre's popular books and patterns created a demand for Irish lace in England and other parts of Europe – a demand that came at just the right time to save lives.

By 1845 Ireland was reeling from a massive famine. A microorganism known as the potato blight had wiped out most of the potato crop that Irish peasants depended on for food. By the time the Irish Potato Famine ended around 1852, more than a million people had died and another million had boarded ships and headed for uncertain lives in the New World.

But some resourceful Irish women and men managed to tap into the demand for Irish lace that Branchardiëre had created. They began eking out a living using their skills as crochet artists, creating a type of lace crochet that became known through Europe as "Irish Crochet." At the same time, Irish crochet workers formed cooperatives and training schools to promote and develop the crochet industry.

Queen Victoria was one the European aristocrats who developed a taste for fine Irish crochet. In her later years she even took up the art herself, crocheting sashes for veterans returning from the Boer War.

A Rich Tapestry

Knitted artifacts exist from as far back as the 11th century but fabrics are fragile and don't last over long periods of time. We know that the art of knitting goes back much farther than that.

Daniel and I are certainly not the first men

Switch to a different ball to have the next wheel a different colour.

3rd rnd: Into any upper right (if right-handed, upper left if left-handed) ch 1 sp before corner, attach with a standing sc, *ch 5, trbp4tog over next 4 sts, ch 5, 1 sc in next ch 1 sp, ch 5, trbp8tog over next 8 tr sts, ch 5,** 1 sc in next ch 1 sp; rep from * twice, then from * to ** once, join. 1 half wheel.

4th rnd: Ch 1, 1 sc in same join st, *(4 tr, ch 1, 4 tr, ch 1, 4 tr) in top of next corner trbp4tog st, 1 sc in next sc st, (4 tr, ch 1, 4 tr) in top of next trbp8tog st,** 1 sc in next sc; rep from * twice, then from * to ** once, join. Break yarn.

I switched to a different ball again to have the next round a different colour and then continued with same ball letting the colour play itself out.

5th rnd: Into any upper right ch 1 sp corner (if right-handed, upper left if left-handed), attach with a standing sc, *ch 5, trbp4tog over next 4 sts, ch 5, [1 sc in next ch 1 sp, ch 5, trbp8tog over next 8 tr sts, ch 5], twice**, 1 sc in next ch 1 sp; rep from * twice, then from * to ** once, join. Break yarn.

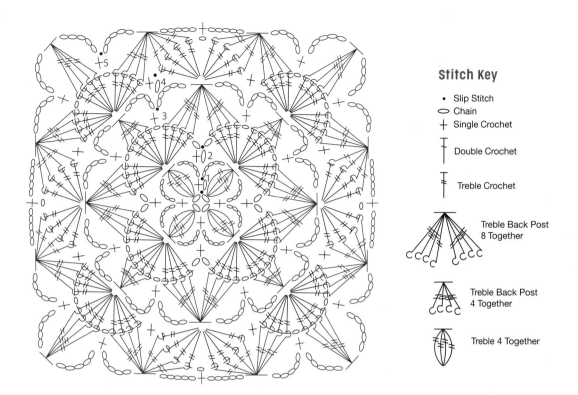

Stitch Key

- • Slip Stitch
- ◯ Chain
- ✛ Single Crochet
- ⊤ Double Crochet
- Ŧ Treble Crochet

Treble Back Post 8 Together

Treble Back Post 4 Together

Treble 4 Together

6th rnd: Attach with sl st in corner st, ch 3 (counts as dc here and throughout), dc in same st, *4 dc in each ch 5 sp to corner st,** (2 dc, ch 2, 2 dc) in corner st; rep from * twice, then from * to ** once, 2 dc in same st as beg, hdc join. 28 dc.

7th rnd: Ch 1, 1 sc in same sp, *1 scbp in each st to corner,** (1 sc, ch 2, 1 sc) in ch 2 sp; rep from * twice, then from * to ** once, 1 sc in beg sp, hdc join. 30 sc.

8th rnd: Ch 1, 1 sc in same sp, *1 sc in each st to corner,** (1 sc, ch 2, 1 sc) in ch 2 sp; rep from * twice, then from * to ** once, 1 sc in beg sp, hdc join. 32 sc.

Slanted Cluster (sl cl) Section

9th rnd: Ch 3, 1 dc in same sp, *sk 2 sts, (3 dc, ch 3, 1 sc) in next st, [sk 3 sts, (3 dc, ch 3, 1 sc) in next st] until 1 st rem before corner, sk next st,** (2 dc, ch 2, 2 dc) in ch 2 sp; rep from * twice, then from * to ** once, 2 dc in beg sp, hdc join. 8 sl cl, 4 dc.

ever to use a single hook and yarn or thread to create something practical or pretty. In fact, the things we call fiber arts today were once considered the almost-exclusive domain of men. The art probably started when hunters and fishermen developed techniques to weave fibres to create nets and snares for hunting and fishing.

The utilitarian practice soon evolved into more pleasant pursuits done more often by women.

There are a few theories as to where crochet originated. Some historians believe it was invented in Arabia and spread throughout Asia and Europe along Arab trade routes. Another theory is that it started in China as an offshoot of a popular form of Chinese needlework. Meanwhile, primitive tribes in South America developed a type of crochet that was independent of the Old World.

However it developed, it wasn't until the Irish explosion, Eleonore Riego de la Branchardière and Queen Victoria that Europeans really got hooked on crochet.

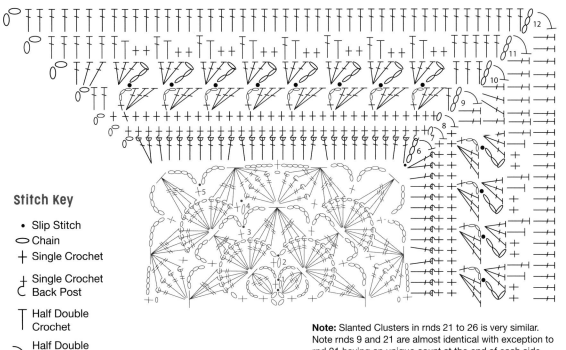

Stitch Key

- • Slip Stitch
- ⬭ Chain
- + Single Crochet
- ⸷ Single Crochet Back Post
- T Half Double Crochet
- ⌐ Half Double Crochet Join
- T Double Crochet
- ⋎ Slanted Cluster Stitches
- ⋏ Slanted Cluster Stitches

Note: Slanted Clusters in rnds 21 to 26 is very similar. Note rnds 9 and 21 are almost identical with exception to rnd 21 having an unique count at the end of each side. Check written instructions for clarification.

10th rnd: Ch 3, 1 dc in same sp, *1 dc in next 2 sts, [sk 3 dc, (sl st, ch 3, 3 dc) in ch 3 sp] until 2 dc rem before corner, sk 2 dc,** (3 dc, ch 2, 2 dc) in ch 2 sp; rep from * twice, then from * to ** once, 3 dc in beg sp, hdc join. 8 sl cl, 7 dc.

11th rnd: Ch 3, 1 dc in same sp, *1 dc in next 4 sts, [1 sc in ch 3 sp, 1 sc in next st, 1 hdc in next st, 1 dc in next st] until 3 sts rem before corner, 1 dc in next 3 sts,** (2 dc, ch 2, 2 dc) in ch 2 sp corner; rep from

* twice, then from * to ** once, 2 dc in beg sp, hdc join. 43 sts.

12th rnd: Ch 3, 1 dc in same sp, *1 dc in each st to corner,** (2 dc, ch 2, 2 dc) in ch 2 sp; rep from * twice, then from * to ** once, 2 dc in beg sp, hdc join. 47 dc.

13th and 14th rnds: As 7th and 8th rnds. 49 sc. 51 sc.

Popcorn Section

15th rnd: Ch 1, 1 sc in same sp, *1 sc in next 9 sts, 1 pc in next st, [1 sc next 15 sts, 1 pc in next st] twice, 1 sc in next 9 sts,** (1 sc, ch 2, 1 sc) in ch 2 sp; rep from * twice, then from * to ** once, 1 sc in beg sp, hdc join. 3 pc, 50 sc.

16th rnd: Ch 1, 1 sc in same sp, *1 sc in next 9 sts, 1 pc in next st, 1 sc in next st, 1 pc in next st, [1 sc in next 13 sts, 1 pc in next st, 1 sc in next st, 1 pc in next st] twice, 1 sc in next 9 sts,** (1 sc, ch 2, 1 sc) in ch 2 sp; rep from * twice, then from * to ** once, 1 sc in beg sp, hdc join. 6 pc, 49 sc.

17th rnd: Ch 1, 1 sc in same sp, *1 sc in next 11 sts, 1 pc in next st, [1 sc in next 15 sts, 1 pc in next st] twice, 1 sc in next 11 sts,** (1 sc, ch 2, 1 sc) in ch 2 sp; rep from * twice, then from * to ** once, 1 sc in beg sp, hdc join. 3 pc, 54 sc.

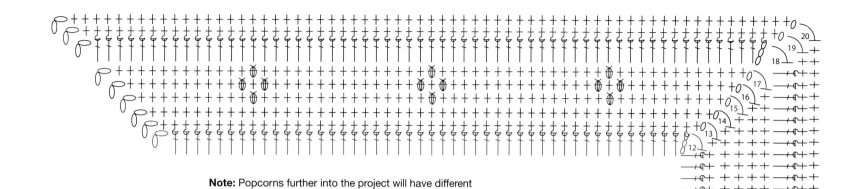

Note: Popcorns further into the project will have different stitch spacing. Check with written pattern for clarification.

18th rnd: As 12th rnd. 61 dc.

19th and 20th rnds: As 7th and 8th rnds. 63 sc. 65 sc.

Slanted Cluster (sl cl) Section

21st rnd: Ch 3, 1 dc in same sp, *sk 2 sts, (3 dc, ch 3, 1 sc) in next st, [sk 3 sts, (3 dc, ch 3, 1 sc) in next st] until 2 sts rem before corner, sk next 2 sts,** (2 dc, ch 2, 2 dc) in ch 2 sp; rep from * twice, then from * to ** once, 2 dc in beg sp, hdc join. 16 sl cl, 4 dc.

22nd rnd: Ch 3, 1 dc in same sp, *1 dc in next 2 sts, [sk 3 dc, (sl st, ch 3, 3 dc) in ch 3 sp] until 2 dc rem before corner, sk 2 dc,** (3 dc, ch 2, 2 dc) in ch 2 sp; rep from * twice, then from * to ** once, 3 dc in beg sp, hdc join. 16 sl cl, 7 dc.

23rd rnd: Ch 3, 1 dc in same sp, *1 dc in next 4 sts, [1 sc in ch 3 sp, 1 sc in next st, 1 hdc in next st, 1 dc in next st] until 3 sts rem before corner, 1 dc in next 3 sts,** (2 dc, ch 2, 2 dc) in ch 2 sp corner; rep from * twice, then from * to ** once, 2 dc in beg sp, hdc join. 75 sts.

24th rnd: As 12th rnd. 79 dc.

25th and 26th rnds: As 7th and 8th rnds. 81 sc. 83 sc.

Bavarian Crochet Section

27th rnd: Ch 4 (counts as tr here and throughout), 3 tr, ch 1, 4 tr in same sp, *sk 5 sts, 1 sc in next st, sk 5 sts, (4 tr, ch 1, 4 tr) in next st, [sk 4 sts, 1 sc in next st, sk 4 sts, (4 tr, ch 1, 4 tr) in next st] until 11 sts rem to corner, sk 5 sts, 1 sc in next st, sk 5 sts,** (4 tr, ch 1, 4

Stitch Key

⌒ Chain
+ Single Crochet

+ Single Crochet
C Back Post

↘ Half Double
  Crochet Join

┬ Double Crochet

 Popcorn

tr, ch 1, 4 tr) in ch 2 sp; rep from * twice, then from * to ** once, 4 tr in beg sp, join with sc to beg ch-4. 7 half wheels, 16 ch 5 sps.

28th rnd: Ch 1, 1 sc in same sp, *ch 5, trbp4tog over next 4 sts, ch 5, 1 sc in next ch 1 sp, [ch 5, trbp8tog over next 8 tr sts, ch 5, 1 sc in next ch 1 sp]**. Rep [ ] to last ch 1 sp before corner; rep from * twice, then from * to ** once, join. 8 half wheels, 18 ch 5 sps.

29th rnd: Ch 1, 1 sc in sc, *(4 tr, ch 1, 4 tr, ch 1, 4 tr) in top of next corner trbp4tog st, 1 sc in next sc st, [(4 tr, ch 1, 4 tr) in top of next trbp8tog st, 1 sc in next sc st]. Rep [ ] to last sc before corner; rep from * twice, then from * to ** once, join. **Break yarn.**

30th rnd: Into any upper right *(if right-handed, upper left if left-handed)* ch 1 sp before corner, attach with a standing sc, *ch 5, trbp4tog over next 4 sts, ch 5, 1 sc in next ch 1 sp, [ch 5, trbp8tog over next 8 tr sts, ch 5, 1 sc in next ch 1 sp]**. Rep [ ] to last ch 1 sp before corner ; rep from * twice, then from * to ** once, join. 9 half wheels, 20 ch 5 sps.

31st and 32nd rnds: As 29th and 30th rnds. 32nd rnd has 10 half wheels, 22 ch 5 sps

33rd rnd: Attach with sl st in corner st, ch 3, *4 dc in next ch 5 sp, [1 dc in next st, 4 dc in next ch 5 sp] to corner st,** (1 dc, ch 2, 1 dc) in corner st; rep from * twice, then from * to ** once, 1 dc in same st as beg, hdc join. 111 dc.

34th and 35th rnds: As 7th and 8th rnds. 113 sc. 115 sc.

Slanted Cluster (sl cl) Section

The next round is not on the diagram as the stitch counts are slightly different.

36th rnd: Ch 3, 1 dc in same sp, *[sk 3 sts, (3 dc, ch 3, 1 sc) in next st] until 3 sts rem before corner, sk next 3 sts,** (2 dc, ch 2, 2 dc) in ch 2 sp; rep from * twice, then from * to ** once, 2 dc in beg sp, hdc join. 28 sl cl, 4 dc.

37th to 41st rnds: As 10th to 14th rnds. 28 sl cl, 7 dc. 123 sts. 127 dc. 129 sc. 131 sc.

Popcorn Section

The next 3 rounds are not on the diagram as the stitch counts are slightly different.

42nd rnd: Ch 1, 1 sc in same sp, *1 sc in next 11 sts, 1 pc in next st, [1 sc next 17 sts, 1 pc in next st] 6 times, 1 sc in next 11 sts,** (1 sc, ch 2, 1 sc) in ch 2 sp; rep from * twice, then from * to ** once, 1 sc in beg sp, hdc join. 7 pc, 126 sc.

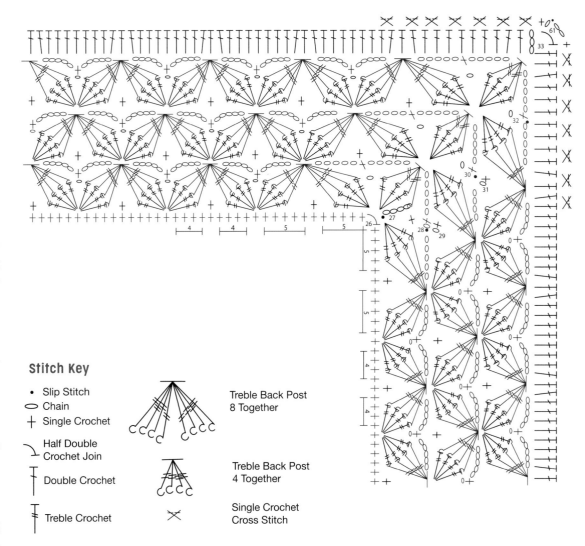

Stitch Key

- • Slip Stitch
- ⬭ Chain
- + Single Crochet
- ⅂ Half Double Crochet Join
- ⊥ Double Crochet
- ‡ Treble Crochet

Treble Back Post 8 Together

Treble Back Post 4 Together

✕ Single Crochet Cross Stitch

From round 34 to the end, refer to the instructions as the stitch counts are slightly different but executed the same way.

46th and 47th rnds: As 7th and 8th rnds. 143 sc. 145 sc.

The next round is not on the diagram as the stitch counts are slightly different.

48th rnd: Ch 3, 1 dc in same sp, *sk 2 sts, (3 dc, ch 3, 1 sc) in next st, [sk 3 sts, (3 dc, ch 3, 1 sc) in next st] until 2 sts rem before corner, sk next 2 sts,** (2 dc, ch 2, 2 dc) in ch 2 sp; rep from * twice, then from * to ** once, 2 dc in beg sp, hdc join. 36 sl cl, 4 dc.

49th to 51st rnds: As 10th to 12th rnds. 36 sl cl, 7 dc. 155 sts. 159 dc.

52nd and 53rd rnds: As 7th and 8th rnds. 161 sc. 163 sc.

Bavarian Section
54th to 60th rnds: As 27th to 33rd rnds. 15 half wheels. 16 half wheels, 34 ch 5 sps. Rnd 56 has no count. 17 half wheels, 36 ch 5 sps. Rnd 58 has no count. 18 half wheels, 38 ch 5 sps. 192 dc.

Border
61st rnd: Ch 1, 1 sc in same sp, *[sk next st, 1 sc in next st, 1 sc in skipped st] to corner,** (1 sc, ch 2, 1 sc) in ch 2 sp; rep from * twice, then from * to ** once, 1 sc in beg sp, ch 2, join. Fasten off. 194 sc.

43rd rnd: Ch 1, 1 sc in same sp, *1 sc in next 11 sts, 1 pc in next st, 1 sc in next st, 1 pc in next st, [1 sc in next 15 sts, 1 pc in next st, 1 sc in next st, 1 pc in next st] 6 times, 1 sc in next 11 sts,** (1 sc, ch 2, 1 sc) in ch 2 sp; rep from * twice, then from * to ** once, 1 sc in beg sp, hdc join. 14 pc, 121 sc.

44th rnd: Ch 1, 1 sc in same sp, *1 sc in next 13 sts, 1 pc in next st, [1 sc in next 17 sts, 1 pc in next st] 6 times, 1 sc in next 13 sts,** (1 sc, ch 2, 1 sc) in ch 2 sp; rep from * twice, then from * to ** once, 1 sc in beg sp, hdc join. 7 pc, 130 sc.

45th rnd: As 12 rnd. 141 dc.

Let's Do Lunch Placemats

Design by By Michael Sellick

Daniel and I always sit down together for lunch and dinner. Throughout the day, we are preoccupied with work, so coming together during these moments allows us to touch base with each other on what is happening both at work and in our own lives.

The screeching of a plate across the table is something that has always driven me crazy. So why not buffer that sound with a soft, cushy placement? Even better when it adds an element of style.

I was inspired by the split-half double crochet stitchwork. It allows you to produce this easy, rectangle shape and you can alter the sizing of the mats to suit your own living experiences. We coloured ours red for the apple orchards that dot the Annapolis Valley where we live, but of course, the colours can be changed to suit your own personal taste.

Each placemat will take 6.3 oz/179 g of yarn. It will take three balls for a set of four.

Materials

Bernat® Maker Home Dec™ (250 g/8.8 oz, 290 m/317 yds) - **Woodberry**, 2 Balls

Use size 8 mm, U.S. L/11 crochet hook or size needed to obtain gauge. Measurement approx 17" [43 cm] long x 12" [30.5 cm] wide. Gauge 9.5 splhdc and 12 rows = 4" [10 cm].

NOTES:
- Ch 1 at beg of the row does not count as st.
- We have a video tutorial for the Split Half Double Stitch if you need more help with visualization.

Ch 33.

1st row: (RS) 1 hdc in 2nd ch from hook. 1 hdc in each ch to end of ch. Turn. 32 hdc.

2nd row: Ch 1. 1 splhdc in each st across. Turn.

Rep last row until work from beg measures approx 17" [43 cm]. Fasten off.

Orchard Wrap

Design by By Michael Sellick

This wrap can be tossed on when you're going casual or when you're dressing to impress. Designed intentionally with an easy repeat, and using a transitional gradient yarn that flows, this pattern cycles through the colour throughout the ball.

If elegance is your style, this wrap's yarn choice lends itself to feeling really special. The lacey effect allows the breeze to blow through without burying you down under a wrap. You wear this wrap, it doesn't wear you.

Start the first ball from the interior and crochet until you get to the end. Begin the next ball from the outside and use the yarn going back to the interior of the ball. For the third ball, start from the interior of the ball once again.

There are three puff sections in total. The first time through, there are only six rows in which you can physically count six puffs climbing up. The second time through, you will be able to count 18 puff stitches. The third time through, there are six puffs once again.

One of the biggest mistakes in doing a wrap is to make it too short, causing the drape and flow of the design to be lost. My wrap was made for the person whose walk matches their flow.

Materials

Red Heart® It's A Wrap Rainbow™ (150 g/5.29, 570 m/623 yds) - **Whisper,** 3 Balls. You will use 2 full balls and 0.67 oz/19 g of the third. Approx 1326 yds/1212 m was used in total.

Use size 4mm, U.S. G/6 crochet hook or size needed to obtain gauge. Measurement approx 90" [228.5 cm] long x 20"[50.5 cm] wide. Gauge 17 sc and 20 rows = 4" [10 cm]. . Measurement approx 90" [228.5 cm] long x 20" [50.5 cm] wide. Gauge 17 sc and 20 rows = 4" [10 cm].

NOTES:

- To change the size, multiples of 6+2.
- There are 66 groups.
- Each group of 6 = 1.25".
- If substituting yarn, it is a fine weight #2 yarn.

Instructions

Ch 398.

1st row: (RS) 1 sc 2nd ch from hook. 1 sc in each ch across. Turn. 397 sts.

2nd row: Ch 1, 1 sc in first st. Ch 6, sk next 5 sts, *1 sc in next st, ch 6, sk next 5 sts. Rep from * across. 1 sc in last st. Turn. 66 ch 6 sps.

3rd row: Ch 1, 1 sc in same beg st. 7 sc in each ch 6 sp across. 1 sc in last st. Turn. 66 groups of 7 sc.

4th row: Ch 7 (counts as 1 tr and ch 3 sp). Sk same st where ch 7 originates plus next 2 sts, 1 sc in next 3 sts. *Ch 6, sk next 4 sts, 1 sc in next 3 sts. Rep from * across until 3 sts are left. Ch 3, 1 tr in last st. Turn. 65 ch 6 groups and 2 half groups on ends.

5th row: Ch 1, 1 sc in same beg st. 3 sc in next ch 3 sp. *Sk next sc, 1 sc in next st, sk next sc. 7 sc in next ch 6 sp. Rep from * across. 3 sc in last ch 3 sp, 1 sc in 4th ch. Turn. 65 - 7 sc groups and 2 half groups on ends.

6th row: Ch 1, 1 sc in first st. Ch 5, sk next 7 sts, *1 sc in next st, ch 5, sk next 7 sts. Rep from * across. 1 sc in last st. Turn. 66 ch 6 gaps.

7th row: Ch 1, 1 sc in same st. * 5 sc in next ch 6 sp. 1 sc in next sc. Rep from * across. Turn. 397 sts.

8th row: Ch 1, 1 sc in each st across. Turn. 397 sts.

9th row puff stitch set-up row: Ch 1, 1 sc in same st. *Ch 3, sk next st, puff st in next, ch 3, sk next 3 sts, 1 sc in next. Rep from * across. Turn. 66 puff sts.

10th row: Ch 2 (doesn't count as st), 1 puff st in same beg st, ch 2, 1 sc in next puff st. Ch 3, puff st in next ch 3 sp. *Ch 3, 1 sc in next puff st, ch 3, puff st in next ch 3 sp. Rep from * across. 1 tr in last st. Turn. 66 puff sts.

11th row: Ch 1, 1 sc in same st. Ch 3, puff st in next ch 3 sp. *Ch 3, 1 sc in next puff st, ch 3, puff st in next ch 3 sp. Rep from * across. Ch 3, 1 sc in last puff st. Turn. 66 puff sts.

12th row: Ch 2 (doesn't count as st), 1 puff st in same beg st, ch 2, 1 sc in next puff st.

After finishing row 20, begin the repeating starting at the top of this list of instructions.

Repeat Rows 9 - 10.

Repeat 11 - 12 (8 times) You will see **18 clusters** in this section.

Repeat Rows 15 - 20

Repeat Rows 9 - 20. You will see **6 clusters** in this section.

Repeat Rows 2 - 5.

Stitch Key

◯ Chain

+ Single Crochet

✒ Puff Stitch

┬ Treble

① Puff Stitch Count

Row 20
Row 19
Row 18
Row 17
Row 16
Row 15
Row 14
Row 13
Row 12
Row 11
Row 10
Row 9
Row 8
Row 7
Row 6
Row 5
Row 4
Row 3
Row 2 WS
Row 1 RS

Multiple: 6 + 2

Repeat

Ch 3, puff st in next ch 3 sp. *Ch 3, 1 sc in next puff st, ch 3, puff st in next ch 3 sp. Rep from * across. 1 tr in last st. Turn. 66 puff sts.

13th and 14th rows: Rep 11th and 12th rows once. You will be able to count 6 puff sts stacked in columns.

In the 15th row, we have to get back to single crochet across. Please watch the first and last group as we need to ensure the balance is restored to 397 sts.

15th row: Ch 1, 1 sc in same st. 1 sc in next puff st, 2 sc in next ch 3 sp. 3 sc in next ch 3 sp. *2 sc in next ch 3 sp, 1 sc in next sc st, 3 sc in next ch 3 sp. Rep from * across until last ch 2 space, making 2 sc into last ch 2 space, 1 sc in last puff st. 1 sc in puff st. Turn. 397 sts.

16th to 20th rows: Ch 1, 1 sc in each st across. Turn. 397 sts.

21st and 22nd rows: Rep 9th and 10th row once.

23rd to 38th rows: Rep 11th and 12th row - 8 times. You will be able to count 18 puff sts stacked in columns when all rows are completed.

39th to 44th rows: Rep 15th to 20th rows once.

45th to 56th rows: Rep 9th to 20th row once.

57th to 60th rows: Rep 2nd to 5th row once. Fasten off and end of the last row.

Setting Up A Successful Craft Show

So you're perfecting your crocheting technique and you're producing a flurry of products that are quickly taking over your house. One great way to clean up space for new projects is to sell some of your inventory at a craft show or flea market.

When we jumped into The Crochet Crowd full-time – and we almost lost everything because of it – I started hitting craft shows to make some money to keep us going. Craft shows can be a great way to get cash in your pocket and to get your work seen by others. But, it's a lot more than wishful thinking. There's a science behind it.

My friend Kathleen Neborah Nolen is a craft show veteran. Here are some of her hints to help make your own foray into the craft show world a big success:

✓ Do your research. You need to understand how each craft show is run and how they plan on advertising it. Does the show have a history of performance? Cost of the show, electricity costs and staging set up may have to match the show's expectations with things like carpet or signage. Where is the show located? Where is your booth

going to be in relation to other vendors? Number of attendees expected? Parking?

✓ Your booth or table setup can really influence your show success. Will the show provide tables and chairs? Will you be inside or outside? Plan for the elements, and be aware that some outdoor shows have restrictions on the type of tents you can use.

✓ The type of show usually influences who will attend. Juried shows usually attract a different clientele and place limits on vendors selling the same items. You have to prove what you are going to sell and stay within boundaries. They can have higher fees, but in Kathleen's experience they often deliver potentially higher returns and exposure, often more than a farmers' market or flea market setups.

✓ Prepare to bring business cards, pens and paper to help you develop repeat customers.

✓ Understand the sweet spot when it comes to setting a price. Kathleen tends to stay within a $3

PRINCE/PRINCESS CROWNS $10

to $60 US range. I say anything over $30 CDN became a decision instead of an impulse cash buy. Have payment options other than cash available. Having a Square card reader to accept debit or credit will significantly change your sales. You can also accept e-transfers by email. There are fees for these services, so suck it up, cash on hand is becoming a thing of the past.

✓ Keep an eye on incidental expenses. Does the show require you to carry insurance, or to purchase it from the show? Should you bring food with you instead of purchasing it at the show to cut down on expenses? Remember that incidental expenses cut into your profits.

✓ Make sure you have enough inventory for the show. Kathleen chooses a limited number of patterns; too many options can be overwhelming for customers. For example, choose a hat pattern and do the hat in several popular colours.

✓ Be aware of the area you're selling in. Do a little research on the local market. Are there local sports teams, school colours, or other geographic differences about this location compared to other regions? And as much as novelty colours are fun to use in projects, solid colours sell more quickly.

✓ Your display is also vital to your success. Have clear and concise pricing signage; use some of your storage containers as part of your display; use shelves or racking systems that are easy to set up.

Yarn Chef Creations
Handcrafted Crochet

✓ Keep an eye out for yarn sales or use craft store coupons to regulate expenses. Value yarn isn't always the best option. Stay in trend with new yarns. Avoid using discontinued colours and yarn. There's a reason why it's discontinued.

✓ Vendor etiquette is to stay out of the way; don't stand in front of the display and block the customer's view of your product. Always say hello, be friendly, don't make it all about you, and let the customer speak. Engage in short talk such as weather or ask engaging questions to invoke a response. The customers will take a moment to stop if they are interested. Watch their body language and respect their decision to move on. Be inspiring, not a salesperson. If you are going to sit there and craft, you might as well just stay home. If your attention is not on the show and customers, you've put up a barrier forcing the customer to get your attention. Meet them halfway by being interested.

✓ Always be friendly with fellow vendors. You can watch displays for others to accommodate restroom breaks and have them return the favour. They are also a good source of information on other upcoming shows.

✓ If you have a registered business, you will need to charge sales tax or factor it into your prices. You

need to know how much tax you have to declare for your report summary at the end of the show. Your yarn supplies and show costs are a deductible business expense. Consult a tax adviser for further advice on this.

✓ Most importantly, have fun! Not all shows are a cash success but making new friends, contacts and socializing is just as important for you mentally and professionally.

YARN TALES: WORLD'S BIGGEST CHRISTMAS STOCKING

A Christmas stocking represents families coming together over the holidays, so it's only natural that the crochet community should come together and build the World's Biggest Christmas Stocking.

We were among the 830 crocheters and knitters from all 50 U.S. states, four Canadian provinces and Ireland who donated the 1,260 squares that made up the project. Each square measured three feet by three feet. When it was finished the Christmas stocking weighed 1,641 pounds. It took 288 balls of yarn and 960 hours of work just to sew it together.

More than $100,000 was raised to buy scholarships through the sales of Caron United Yarn, with 15 cents per ball going directly to Children of Fallen Patriots Foundation for scholarships for children who have lost a parent in the line of duty. The afghan squares were removed from the stocking and given to those in need of comfort and warmth.

The World's Biggest Christmas Stocking was unveiled in Fayetteville, North Carolina, on December 8, 2015, and recognized by Guinness World Records as the largest crocheted or knitted Christmas stocking in history. It measured 76 feet wide by 136 feet long and used 5,940 balls of yarn.

This is one of many ways that crocheters can come together in unity to support the causes they feel strongly about.

116

Abbreviations

Below is a long list of common abbreviations as well as descriptions for special stitches that go beyond basics.

Approx Approximately

Beg Begin(ing)

Beg Sunset Reflection St Ch 3, 1 tr in same st (counts as 1), skip 2 sts, place tr4tog by placing 2 of the tog stitches in the next st, skip next 2 stitches, place next 2 tog stitches in the next st. Yoh and pull through 6 loops on hook.

Bet Between

Big V-st(s) Big V-stitch(es). 1 dc, ch 3, 1 dc using same st.

Bp Back post

Blo Back loop only

Bpdc Back post double crochet

Break At the end of each round where the colour is going to be changed. Break means to end the colour, fasten off and weave in ends. It's assumed you are breaking the same colour being used in the round.

Bs Bean stitch

Ch Chain

Cluster (Yoh and insert into stitch, yoh and pull through stitch, yoh pull through 2 loops.) 4 times. 5 loops on hook, yoh and pull through all 5 loops.

Cr dcfp Cross Double Crochet Front Post. Miss next dc. Dcfp around post of next dc, then dcfp around post of missed dc.

Dbl Double

Dtr Double treble

Dtrcl Double Treble Cluster, Yoh twice and draw up a loop in next stitch. (Yoh and draw through 2 loops on hook) twice. Yoh twice and draw up a loop in same stitch. (Yoh and draw through 2 loops on hook) twice. Yoh and draw through all 3 loops on hook.

Dc Double crochet

Dc2tog Double crochet 2 stitches back post (Yoh and draw up a loop in next stitch. Yoh and draw through 2 loops on hook) twice. Yoh and draw through all loops on hook.

Dcbp Double crochet back post. Yoh and draw up a loop around post of stitch at back of work, inserting hook from right to left. (Yoh and draw through 2 loops on hook) twice.

Dcfp Double crochet front post Yoh and draw up a loop around post of stitch at front of work, inserting hook from right to left. (Yoh and draw through 2 loops on hook) twice.

Dec Decrease

Ea Each

Ex sc Extended single crochet

Ex ex sc Extended extended single crochet. Insert hook into st, yoh, pull through, yoh, pull through 1 loop, yoh, pull through next loop, yoh, pull through final 2 loops.

Fig Figure 1 (picture of stitch)

Flat Petal St (1 tr, 5 dc, 1 tr) in same st. This stitch spans over 8 stitches.

FLO Front loop only

FP Front post

FPdc Front post double crochet

Gr Group

Hdc Half double crochet

Hdc Join Half double crochet join to the top of the beg ch or st.

Inc Increase

Join At the end of a round, join to the beginning stitch or top of a beginning chain with a slip stitch.

Ldc Long double crochet

Lp(s) Loop(s)

Lsc Long single crochet

MC Main color

Pat Pattern

Pc st Popcorn stitch, see pattern for definitions as not a standard stitch or count.

Picot Ch 3. Sl st back into last sc worked.

Prev Previous

Puff St Puff stitch, (Yoh and Insert hook into assigned stitch or space. Yoh, draw through stitch or sp, yoh and through 2 loops on hook.) 3 times. Yoh and draw through 3 loops only, leaving the last 2 loops on hook. Yoh and draw through the last 2 loops.

Rem Remaining

Rep Repeat

Rnd(s) Round(s)

RS right side

Rsc Reverse single crochet

Sc Single crochet

Scbp Single crochet back post

Scfp Single crochet front post

Shark Fin St 1 sc, ch 2, sk next 2 sts, 1 tr in next. Ch 3, 6 dc along the tr post. Sk next 2 sts.

Shell Is the number of stitches that form a fan shape. It can be defined in multiples of ways. Refer to the pattern for specifics.

Sk Skip

Sl cl Slanted cluster, sk 3 sts, (3 dc, ch 3, 1 sc) in next st.

Sl st Slip stitch

Sp(s) Space(s)

Spec Tog St 1 dc + 1 hdc together as a st. The dc will use the next empty or assigned stitch 2 rnds below by going over top of the ch 1 completely so the ch 1 is encased inside the dc. Then use the next hdc st in rnd below to bring them together.

Splhdc Split half double crochet, work hdc between 'legs' at front and back of stitch (splitting stitch) instead of through top loops.

St(s) Stitch(es)

Standing Sc Form slip knot and insert onto the hook. Insert hook into st, yoh and pull loop through, yoh through 2 loops.

Sunset Reflection St Tr6tog spanning over the next 7 stitches. Place 2 tr stitches in first st, skip 2 sts, place 2 stitches in next st, skip 2 stitches, place last 2 stitches in next st. Yoh and pull through all 7 loops.

Tog Together

Tr Treble

Tr2tog Treble crochet 2 together, *Yoh twice and draw up a loop in next stitch. (Yoh and draw through 2 loops on hook) twice. Repeat from * once. Yoh and draw through all 3 loops on hook.

Tr4tog Treble crochet 4 together, *Yoh twice and draw up a loop in next stitch. (Yoh and draw through 2 loops on hook) twice. Repeat from * once. Yoh and draw through all 3 loops on hook.

Trbp4tog Treble crochet back post 4 together, *Yoh twice and draw up a loop around post of stitch at back of work, inserting hook from right to left. (Yoh and draw through 2 loops on hook) twice. Repeat from * 3 more times. Yoh and draw through all 5 loops on hook.

Trbp8tog Treble crochet back post 8 together, *Yoh twice and draw up a loop around post of stitch at back of work, inserting hook from right to left. (Yoh and draw through 2 loops on hook) twice. Repeat from * 7 more times. Yoh and draw through all 9 loops on hook.

Trbp Treble back post, Yoh twice and draw up a loop around post of stitch at back of work, inserting hook from right to left. (Yoh and draw through 2 loops on hook) three times.

Trfp2tog Treble crochet front post 2 together, *Yoh twice and draw up a loop around post of stitch at front of work, inserting hook from right to left. (Yoh and draw through 2 loops on hook) twice. Repeat from * once. Yoh and draw through all 3 loops on hook.

Trfp Treble front post, Yoh twice and draw up a loop around post of stitch at front of work, inserting hook from right to left. (Yoh and draw through 2 loops on hook) three times.

WS wrong side

X-st Skip next st or sp, dc in next st or sp, dc in skipped st or sp.

Xsc Skip the 1st st, 1 sc in next st. 1 sc in the skipped st and directly over the first st to bury it.

Yo(h) Yarn over or yarn over hook

Remember that abbreviations are used like regular punctuation of a sentence. Capitalization matches the sentence structure. Here's an example:

> **3rd row:** *Ch 3, counts as dc here and throughout. 1 dc in each st across. Turn.*

Tunisian Abbreviations

Bind Off Insert hook into the vertical bar of the next stitch. Yarn over and pull through the two loops on the hook. Repeat until the end of the row.

Ch Chain stitch

FwP Forward pass

Loh Loop(s) on hook

Lp(s) Loop(s)

Rep Repeat

RetP Return pass, Yo, draw through the first loop on the hook, * Yo, draw through next 2 lps, rep from * across until 1 lp remains.

Sk Skip

Sl St Slip Stitch

St(s) Stitch(es

Tfs Tunisian full stitch, Insert hook from front to back under horizontal bar between two sts, yo and pull up a loop.

Tss Tunisian simple stitch, Insert hook from right to left under next vertical bar, yo and pull up a lp.

Tss2tog Tss together, Insert hook from right to left under next 2 vertical bars, yo, and draw through 2 loops on hook.

Yo Yarn over

Terms & Common Measurements

Information from the Craft Yarn Council.

" or **in** Inch

cm Centimeter

dia Diameter

g Gram

m Meter

mm Millimeter

oz Ounce

yd(s) Yard(s)

* Repeat the instructions following the single asterisk as directed.

** Repeat instructions between the asterisks as many times as directed or repeat at specified locations.

{ } Work instructions within the brackets as many times as directed.

[ ] Work instructions within the brackets as many times as directed.

( ) Work instructions within parentheses as many times as directed or work a group of stitches all in the same stitch or space.

Resources: Join the Crowd

Since we started our *YouTube* channel, we have always worked hard to provide a full slate of resources for everyone from beginners to advanced crochet artists. Matching projects with videos can be found on our website, TheCrochetCrowd.com. Many stitch samples and basic tutorials are also available when you need help.

Whether your project is a scarf with a simple pattern or an elaborate picture blanket, you can use our tutorials to guide your way through. It's like crocheting along with a good friend.

Projects on the website are sorted in a number of ways:

- Level of complexity
- Pattern category
- Technique
- Theme
- Occasions
- Yarn Brand

We've also broken up some of the larger projects into chapters, to make them less daunting and also so that The Crochet Crowd community can work on projects together. We are a community, after all.

Playlists are updated each time a new video is added to *YouTube*, which is daily in some cases. On our website you will find an organized category list to help you easily locate the project that is perfect for your skills and interests. Each link will take you directly to the *YouTube* tutorial you're looking for.

These videos will get you started or help you get to the next level with your crochet project.

A great place to start is to join us on *Facebook*. There you can get the latest updates on new patterns and Stitch Along events. Come on in and explore all the resources that The Crochet Crowd has to offer.

The Pattern Testing Team

The team has pulled together to not only assist with the instructions of this book, but also the countless free patterns we have offered over the years. Some of our featured designers have also tested along the way as well.

Diane Suder

Living in Texas in the winter and in Michigan in summer, Diane is one of the individuals I have known the longest in the yarn arts. If you have ever picked up the Entrelac technique with my teaching, you can thank Diane for showing me how.

Diane quickly jumped forward to become the leader of our closed captioning team. She has subtitled the majority of our tutorials so that deaf and hard of hearing community members have access.

The closed captioning team has also opened The Crochet Crowd to more languages across the world through *YouTube*.

Cathy Lund

As a lover of all things creative, she is not only an experienced crocheter, but also knitter, sewer, painter and gardener (we're just going to stop there.) We met Cathy at a quilting group years ago where I was a guest speaker. To Daniel and me, she's not only part of the team, she's family.

Don't ask her about winning third prize in a baking contest. She'll have long excuses. We ate it for dessert and it tasted like first prize!

Donna Bondy

She makes many clothing pieces for herself. Donna is a rebel when it comes to yarn and she is fully immersed in the yarn arts.

In love with the colouring of variegated yarn, she loves appreciates the colour changing hues and the unexpected story that can come out of a project by using with the colours to their best advantage she plays with. Donna has won the fastest crocheter on the cruise ship TWICE, and blindfolded crochet too! Don't ask about the water sprinkler in her cabin as there is a reason she invented the water sprinkler dance!

Crocheting
keeps me from
Unravelling

Wendy Marple

In the testing of *Study of The Journey* Afghan, the colours she chose were reflective of trying to find joy during difficult times. Wendy has tested many designs for us over the years. She prefers projects with milestones versus crocheting the same thing over and over. Her attention to the smallest details is simply incredible.

Her cat is called Jet. Of course, it's jet black and blends into the darkness. She playfully challenges herself to find Jet in the dark.

Michele Sanders

Michele is quick to edit the wording and sees obvious mistakes right off the hop. She's the person you want on an excursion just for fun. She has a room full of yarn and is ready to test future designs. Time is always a factor for the testing team.

Michele is a dedicated *yarnie* and even named her cat Bernat (Bernie for short). She is affectionately known as the Colorado crocheter and teaches crocheting at her local craft store.

Nancy Elliott

Nancy caught my eye during the launch of the Flora Afghan. She did up the first square as an entire afghan and it looked like the 70s Dating Game. Her speed was incredible. I mean, this "hooker" is a crochet machine.

If we need something tested, I swear to God she has a hook with her and yarn ready to go. We met briefly at a live show in Toronto. She gifted me the afghan which hangs as part of our studio decor

Other Thanks

In appreciation of the opportunities along our journey, I would also like to extend a warm thank you for all their help to Rita Gramsch, Stuart Hochwert, Michelle McDonald, Ryan Newell, Denise Darragh and Liz Ridout, to name a few.

My design skills can be tributed to observation on how to write patterns, and then practising over time. Spinrite design mentors are Svetlana Avrakh, Gayle Bunn, Nicole Winer, Katherine Poole-Fournier, Erin Black and Julia Madill, to name a few. They have helped me steer my boat when I felt off course.

Special shout out to our crochet cruises agent, Sherry Leybovich. She is the fearless leader and life 'buoy' we needed at the negotiations table. Her excellence in customer support keeps our floating conferences sailing along, and wouldn't have been possible without her.

Wendy Maruna is top level when it comes to memory and watching over our communities to keep a safe space. It's unbelievable what she can remember and though it's handy, it's sometimes a curse.

Follow Us

on *Facebook, YouTube*
and our Website!

www.thecrochetcrowd.com
https://www.facebook.com/TheCrochetCommunity
https://www.facebook.com/groups/TheCrochetCrowdStitchSocial
https://www.instagram.com/thecrochetcrowd